The Writing Shop

Teaching Writing

Scope

The *Teaching Writing* series publishes concise instructional writing guides. Series books each focus on a different subject area, discipline or type of writing. The books are intended to be used in undergraduate and graduate courses across the disciplines and can also be read by individual researchers or students engaged in thesis work.

Series authors must have a demonstrated publishing record and must hold a PhD, MFA or the equivalent. Please email queries to the series editor at pleavy7@aol.com

VOLUME 7

The Writing Shop

Putting 'Shop' Back in Writing Workshop

By

Suzanne Farrell Smith

BRILL

SENSE

LEIDEN | BOSTON

All chapters in this book have undergone peer review.

The Library of Congress Cataloging-in-Publication Data is available online at
http://catalog.loc.gov

ISSN 2542-9698
ISBN 978-90-04-39601-2 (paperback)
ISBN 978-90-04-39787-3 (hardback)
ISBN 978-90-04-39788-0 (e-book)

This book is printed on acid-free paper and produced in a sustainable manner.

ADVANCE PRAISE FOR
THE WRITING SHOP

"Filled with illuminating quotes and inspiring anecdotes, *The Writing Shop* is potent, simple, and persuasive. It pulled the writer in me back to my notebooks and fueled the teacher in me to refresh the classrooms I work in. A necessary and timely reminder about the importance of authenticity."
– Dorothy Barnhouse, international literacy consultant, author of *Readers Front and Center*, and co-author of *What Readers Really Do*

"I was given an advance copy of Suzanne Farrell Smith's book *The Writing Shop* and I was thrilled to see her promote a refocusing of our work with writers that embraces the brilliance of a shop model. Suzanne believes that just like when learning a craft or trade, a shop is the most engaging environment in which to be mentored, to experiment, and to practice the craft of writing. The human element of developing trusting and nurturing relationships between master and apprentice is central to the premise of her work. She shares anecdotes from her personal life and from real-world experiences of craftsmen to illuminate her ideas and the elements of shop. Suzanne advocates for a playful and stimulating learning environment, without compromising academic expectations. Come take a peek inside her shop and learn from a master!"
– Paula Bourque, literacy coach and author of *Close Writing: Developing Purposeful Writers in Grades 2–6* and *Quick Writing: Nurturing Hearts and Minds in Elementary Classrooms*

"*The Writing Shop* is rich. Rich in storytelling, rich in detail, rich in imagery, rich in inspiration. I challenge any teacher reading this book to not be inspired and renewed with a fresh sense of what is possible when children are allowed to play in the process of writing. In *The Writing Shop*, Suzanne continues a tradition of master teachers generously sharing their hard-earned insight into how teachers can help children steward the shop that is their own imagination and voice. Teachers tasked with helping children master the craft of writing would do well to add this immensely useful and beautiful text to their shelf."
– Nancy Cavillones, writer and former New York City English teacher

"Reading Suzanne Farrell Smith's *The Writing Shop* is like embarking on a journey of the senses, where one finds oneself immediately endeared to her lovely vision of what writing workshop could be. With frequent nods to the value that play, noise, and "mess" can bring to any kind of workshop, Suzanne reminds us to slow down and enjoy not just the products that students ultimately create, but their beautiful and varying processes as well—for this is where the true magic of writing workshop happens."

– **Shawna Coppola, author of** *RENEW! Become a Better—and More Authentic—Writing Teacher*

"This beautiful, approachable book not only teaches you how to teach writing, but reclaims the rightful place of "shop" in writing workshop. Suzanne Farrell Smith captures how it should feel for anyone of any age to write: full of exploration, spontaneity, and joy. *The Writing Shop* is the perfect blend of teaching strategies, student stories, and Suzanne's own personal journey in becoming a teacher of writing and, more importantly, of writers. Novel in its approach and singular in its voice, *The Writing Shop* is a must-read book that will undoubtedly make your classroom and your students come alive through the writing process. Every child deserves the kind of writing shop classroom Suzanne will help you create."

– **Katie Egan Cunningham, Associate Professor at Manhattanville College and author of** *Story: Still the Heart of Literacy Learning* **and** *Happiness by Design*

"Real writing is messy business. Rarely do writers churn out perfect works by following a linear, five-step writing process to a T. Why then do we expect our students to perform this way? In *The Writing Shop*, Suzanne Farrell Smith masterfully breaks down the barriers of product-focused writing instruction and invites teachers to let their students explore the messy business of writing as a craft. Beautifully woven among tidbits and tales of her own young writing students, Suzanne's detailed, specific suggestions for integrating the essential components of a creative shop into a classroom are perfect for both the novice and the experienced teacher, for those just starting to integrate a workshop model to those who are looking for ways to reinvigorate an existing writing workshop. Best of all, Suzanne focuses on the fun of writing and ignites (or reignites!) an excitement that is essential for any teacher looking to inspire students to find, develop, and hone the skills that make writing messy and real and wonderful."

– **Jenni Eaton, writer, English teacher at Takoma Park Middle School and Adjunct Associate Professor of Writing at University of Maryland University College**

"*The Writing Shop* connects to the roots of a true workshop and helps us understand that writing is an art of playful making and doing. Suzanne takes concepts like 'living like a writer' and makes them crystal clear by weaving in personal stories, teaching stories, and research. Reading this book is a gift to any teacher who wants to ensure that shop is a big part of their writing workshop and that students and teachers alike feel energized and authentically engaged in writing."
– Gravity Goldberg, literacy consultant and author of *Teach Like Yourself*

"In *The Writing Shop*, educators will find a blueprint for creating a workshop in which students learn the fundamentals of composition with glee rather than dread, that inspires reluctant writers to experiment and play, and facilitates student leadership, competence, and confidence. Writers will find a guide for revolutionizing the writing desk, as well as the practice of writing. With a warm, clear, compassionate voice, Suzanne invites readers to join her in approaching writing as a messy, joyful experiment. Part history, part memoir, part how-to, this book is a celebration of the written word. It is the kind of book you will carry around in your back pocket and, in no small part because of Suzanne's keen insight and wisdom, the kind of book that becomes a mentor and a friend."
– Sarah Twombly, writer and Adjunct Professor at Husson University

To Sebastian, Josiah, and Rafferty

May you always build meaningful things.

CONTENTS

ACKNOWLEDGEMENTS

Thank you to Dr. Patricia Leavy, for your belief in and commitment to *The Writing Shop*, as well as everyone at Brill | Sense.

Thank you to all the teacher-writers I've known. Emphatic thanks to Katie Egan Cunningham, my remarkable friend and role model, who encouraged me to develop this book.

To all my students past and present—at Grace Church School, Saint David's School, Thomas A. Edison School, the GO Project, Escuela San Luis de Florencia, LIM College, and Manhattanville College—you make me love teaching writing. Special thanks to those who, with their families, allowed me to share their photographs and stories.

Matt Casey at the Carver Center, thank you for your invaluable help. Sarah Twombly, thank you for remembering our conversation and sending me a lead. The team at Miller-Driscoll School, thank you for inspiring me and nurturing my children.

I am grateful to the shop masters who welcomed visits, surveys, and conversations, especially Bob Boyce, Eric Dixon, Jenni Eaton, Chris Farrell, Beth Sullivan, Cheryl Wilder, and Danielle Wolf.

And thank you to my husband, Justin. Your sweeping support is everything.

INTRODUCTION

One stunning April morning, I left my twin toddler boys with a trusted babysitter, dropped my older son off at preschool to sing and play the morning away, and drove across Westchester County, New York, to visit the Jacob Burns Film Center. A colleague at Manhattanville College, where I am an adjunct professor in the literacy department, had connected me with the Burns Center's director of education, because she knew we shared beliefs about literacy education as well as similar family lives: we both have twins and we both recently moved our families from New York to Connecticut. Our plan was to get to know each other and swap ideas about twenty-first-century literacy. I enjoyed every minute of the solo drive that let me listen to a social science podcast, rather than my sons' beloved Wiggleworms album.

The moment I entered the film center's lobby, something caught my eye. An open door beyond the elevator revealed a crowded but organized theater workshop. Two-by-fours, power tools, and all manner of rivets and screws waited to be selected and used. I was told third graders would be along soon to continue building sets for films they were making.

Days later, I could not get this workshop out of my head. The smell alone—damp, woody, a little metallic—drew me to my childhood home, where my father's basement workshop was chock-full of projects in progress. Workbenches along all four walls were hidden under chisels, planes, and tape measures. Cabinets that had been dragged home from local yard sales were stuffed with specialty parts. Shelves of scraps, mostly wood and metal, threatened to tip under the weight. A vise, bolted to one of the smaller benches, waited with steel jaws wide open.

My father's workshop was all-purpose. Down in the shop, he tinkered with appliances. He built model ships, ones he'd begun while serving on a Naval submarine during the Vietnam War. And he created delightful features for his model train display, like miniature blowtorches and spinning spotlights. One shop corner was designated a darkroom, where he processed his own black-and-white photographs. All was possible because at his fingertips were different work surfaces, materials, and tools.

My father died when I was six—killed in a head-on collision with a drunk driver—and I don't remember him. But I know the workshop, because my grieving mother, a seamstress with her own tiny shop, did not alter a single thing after his death. It reminded her too much of her husband. For years, my sisters tell me, we played in the suspended space. We glued rough wood pieces into dollhouse furniture and counted the glass jars he'd nailed to the ceiling to hold small parts like washers and wires. The workshop was our connection to our father. Surrounded by sensory reminders, down to the hum of the mini-fridge in the corner still cooling cans of Budweiser, we could tap our shared history while doing what he loved to do: build.

Figure 1. My sisters and I play "ballet dancers" in our father's workshop

Shop is in my blood. My great-aunt sewed baseballs for the major leagues, long before the operation moved overseas (where the balls are still stitched by hand). My grandmother stamped golf balls. And my grandfather built radios; in his basement, down narrow wooden stairs that creaked under our little bare feet, was a machine shop with electric trains and metal shelves lined with my grandmother's pickling jars. My siblings, aunts, uncles, and cousins devote their hands and ideas to everything from greeting cards to classic cars. Many are scratch cooks. For my sisters and me, childhood free time was spent playing with toys and practicing piano in our basement, in the space between our mother's sewing studio and our father's workshop.

I spent my teen years working at a gift shop in Connecticut, close to Mystic Seaport. When I could pay the entrance fee, I'd roam the museum grounds, lingering by the boat-building workshop, where students were taught to use traditional tools to build miniature seaworthy boats. "Learn by doing!" the flyers advertised. Mystic Seaport is still known for its hands-on workshops about boats and beyond, from period costumes to nineteenth-century stationery. Whenever I come across a workshop like this, I tend to spend as much time in it as I'm allowed. Workshops fascinate me. Where a thing is made, I want to observe. How a thing is made, I want to know.

The open workshop door at the film center opened a whole lot more for me. I instantly related what third graders were doing in that shop to what I would be discussing in my meeting upstairs: writing instruction. Everything I believe about writing, and the teaching of writing, jumped out to me in full relief. I have always loved writing in a shop.

There's a reason we—adults and children alike—love shop. We get to build stuff. We walk in the door and don distinct outfits—aprons, smocks, goggles, gloves—shifting mode both physically and mentally. We hear the sound of machines and take in a variety of smells and grip heavy tools in our hands. We pair up differently and talk in specialized vocabulary. We feel vibrations in our arms as we hammer, sand, thread, and latch. We sense our own power as we wield tools and materials to make, from disparate parts, meaningful things. Shop excites. Shop delights. Shop says move, use your hands, collaborate.

The Writing Shop is based on the premise that just as any shop is the most practical and enjoyable environment in which to learn and practice a trade or craft, a writing workshop that remembers its roots as a shop is the most practical and enjoyable environment in which to learn and practice the writing craft.

The writing workshop model, developed in the 1970s and growing more and more popular in today's schools, is a highly effective way to teach writing. This book, rather than arguing that claim, expands on it. There can be no doubt that writing workshop is powerful; however, despite best teaching practices and the openness to new ideas and thinking on our feet required by the workshop model, we writers and writing teachers still hone in on the end product. This makes sense. Complete projects are, by nature, part of the life of a workshop. Photographers send out finished prints to display on walls, publish in books, and hang in galleries. Architects erect models to use as three-dimensional building blueprints. Theater technicians craft stage sets against which new worlds come to life. So too does a writing workshop turn out final products: the pieces of writing that inform, persuade, and move readers. In order to balance product with process, we offer our students robust scaffolds, elaborate graphic organizers, intense coaching, step-by-step guidance, and line editing, all to transport them from seed idea to final draft. Because we're good at that. And because we believe our students (and their families) demand it.

But sometimes, in our eagerness to shuttle our students through the writing process to the final product, we forget how important it is to play, make mistakes, change direction, and discover along the way. We forget how acceptable, even preferable, it is to leave things some things in the shop unfinished.

Perhaps you are reading this book for an undergraduate course on literacy instruction. Perhaps you are a graduate student in a course on writing workshop. Perhaps you are a working teacher engaged in professional development to strengthen your literacy block or workshop structure. You may be here to shake up your own writing routine. Whatever path led you to this book, I hope to show you how to put shop back in writing workshop.

I invite you to peek inside workshops of all kinds and borrow their elements for your writing workshop. I want writing shops to smell and sound and feel dynamic like their fellow shops do, with a little noise, a little mess. I want teachers who have not yet adopted the workshop model to consider how shop elements can still enrich any program of writing instruction.

I want you to see yourself as a master craftsperson. In a writing shop, teachers wade deep into writing along with their students and capitalize on their inherent love of the written word. These teacher-writers recognize that they are more than capable of guiding their students on the path to mastery of the writing craft.

I urge you to participate in writing with all your senses and interests. I want teachers and students alike to immerse in a variety of writing materials, wield the tools of writing, and try new techniques in molding, crafting, building. I want writers to enter writing workshop the way they enter a darkroom or test kitchen, woodshop or art studio: breathing in the work of writing, ready to engage in the process, willing to learn new skills and apply them, all under the guidance of a master. These are the students who will write across the curriculum and in their personal lives. These are the students who, as they grow, rather than let fly the uninformed comment or post or email, will thoughtfully assess and compose. These are the students who will see themselves as writers with the power and the right to participate in society. These are the students who will effect change.

Can our writing workshops perfectly mirror arts and industrial workshops? A writing workshop can't, of course, actually smell, look, feel like a woodshop or a sculpture studio. Purposes, tools, and materials all change from shop to shop. Writers build with ideas and words, not planks and nails. But if we look closely at various workshops, we can name the common elements that make them so exciting to young learners and infuse our writing workshops with those elements. This book allows teacher-writers to do just that: visit workshops, identify their core elements, and apply those elements to their writing shops.

Chapter 1, "The Drafting Table," gives a brief history of the writing workshop model. Chapter 2, "Building the Argument," lays out three primary reasons that writing workshops should incorporate the elements of shop: shop reinstates exploratory play as a central component of learning to write; shop invites all types of learners to write, including English language learners, students with special needs, and students who show reluctance toward writing; and shop supports the development and practice of off-page skills. Chapters 3–9 discuss the seven shop elements: master, mess, sense stimulation, workspace variety, safety procedures, technical skills, and craft techniques. Chapter 10, "Share the Masterpiece," offers ideas for publication that result naturally from a writing shop.

Ten years after I founded a New-York-City-based writing salon called Salon Esse, fellow members Caitlin Leffel and Crystal Mandler (2016) compiled the decade's most memorable pieces. To open the collection, they describe Salon Esse as a space that demands the creation of millions of sentences. *The Writing Shop* asks you to look carefully at where writing happens and to consider how to make it a space that invites, even *demands*, the creation of millions of sentences.

THE DRAFTING TABLE

Writing is important in children's lives because it enables them to pay attention to the world, make sense of the planet, improve the quality of their lives, and hold on to their childhoods. (Harwayne, 2000, p. 47)

My three older sisters and I grew up in a single-zip-code village in southeastern Connecticut. Many of our neighbors worked shifts in Connecticut's shoreline industry: Electric Boat, Pfizer, DOW Chemical. Our father was in the Navy, which brought him and my mother to the area, home of an important Navy base. On a brand-new street, they built a small house, which they expanded and expanded again until it suited their needs. My mother was a middle-school math teacher before having us girls, year by year, all in a row. Trained in fabric at a young age by her mother, she retired from teaching and became a seamstress, sewing for the priests at her church and hemming for families with fast-growing children. In her basement shop, she crafted holiday decorations, tooth-fairy pillows, baby bibs, bags for yoga mats, pet cushions, dresses for her daughters, and just about anything else that was asked of her. My sisters and I attended a parochial nursery program, then enrolled in the town's public K–6 school.

As it happens, I don't remember this childhood. My family suffered two significant tragedies—my father's death in a head-on collision with a drunk driver when I was in kindergarten, and a fire that nearly destroyed our family home a few weeks into my third-grade year. While my sisters retained their memories, I, the youngest, lost mine. I don't remember my teachers, classrooms, routines, or friends. I can't recall what it was like to learn math facts or build projects for social studies class. Even when pressed, I couldn't name a favorite food, sweater, holiday, board game, or book from my childhood. My memory before age 12 is virtually blank.

When my mother died in 2015, my sisters and I faced the immense task of emptying her home, the one she and my father built together, in order to sell it. My mother was a packrat. She kept everything, especially after the fire. She kept each ornament, each science activity, and each well-worn toy. She stuck notes to our school papers and projects, begging us to save them. While cleaning the house, we pulled our childhood from every closet and corner. I inherited a storage locker full of boxes, overstuffed because childhood projects tend to be three-dimensional, folded at odd angles, and quite wrinkled.

Evidence of my childhood writing is scattered throughout. Each report card lists my writing skills in terms of whether I mastered grammar and punctuation. All my spelling quizzes are sheets of paper cut into strips, with numbered lists of words divorced from contextual meaning. Scores are circled in red near my name. Grammar worksheets demonstrate that I could add end punctuation to pre-written sentences. Lined papers show individuals letters written over and over and over again for practice. My simple stories are printed on oversized sheets with open space for illustrations.

Figure 1.1. One of my writing projects from first grade

Such was the way writing was taught when I was a child. Writing was split into component parts, each one isolated within the covers of a workbook: vocabulary, spelling, grammar, and penmanship. When it came time to write a piece—and I doubt the word "piece," which hints at high-brow arts, was even used back then—students were given an assignment, a model, and parameters. We were expected to carry over spelling and grammar, to use at least one new vocabulary word from the week. I'm sure we were told to write neatly with a proper grip. Our final copies were starred, points off for sloppiness and misspellings. Every letter stroke was in pencil.

It saddens me that the whole record of my childhood writing—final copies my teachers felt were worthy of sending home—shows nothing of my childlike thought process. The late poet Max Ritvo (2016) once said, "Poetry is great at showing how a mind works, the way a bunch of different images will be clattering all around and suddenly braid together into a metaphor at the last minute." Similarly, when describing the writing process of a young student named Alison, researcher Donald Graves (1983) writes, "What Alison doesn't know is that what reaches the page is the end result of a long line of reductions from an original swirl of memories ..." (p. 219). As the mother of three young boys, I want nothing more than to return to my childhood mind, to connect my past with their present, to dive inside the clattering and swirling that led to my written stories and look for lessons I can share with my children. But I can't review on paper how my young brain worked. And without childhood memory, I'm cut off from that mind completely. The writing is flat, the product is flat. Even the pictures are flat.

Figure 1.2. Spelling quiz from elementary school

Think back to composition classes in your earlier years of education. What did writing look like in school? Did you fold your paper lengthwise for spelling quizzes and fill in punctuation marks on language arts workbook pages? Did you ever free-write stories and poems, or was your writing tied specifically to curriculum goals: write a sentence about frogs, write a paragraph about winter, write a letter to your mother for Mother's Day? Did you write every day or once a week or not at all? Were you given time to write something on your mind—whether or not it was neat, organized, and spelled correctly? Were you granted time with your teacher to talk about your work as a writer?

As my sisters and I were growing through grade school, a revolution was taking place in the world of writing education. By the early 1970s, Donald Graves was a doctoral candidate at the University of Buffalo, doing research on how children learn to write. In 1976, Graves founded the Writing Process Laboratory at the University of New Hampshire. Writing curriculum as process instruction, rather than a method to get to final products, was also born.

Graves and his contemporaries lifted the components of writing out of the traditional curricular sections and united them. Writing instruction as a series of isolated fill-in-the-blank exercises to practice technical skills—the method by which I learned to write—was now deemed the *former* method. Writing instruction as a way to help students make meaning, express themselves, observe closely, think critically about the world, and discover personal and universal truths, grew into the new fashion, at least for those teachers and schools willing to risk retooling their writing programs.

Graves prioritized choice, authentic audiences, mentor texts, and daily time for writing. He embedded, rather than separated, the elements of composition: sentence structure, paragraphs, word choice, spelling, grammar, punctuation, even handwriting. He argued that while most writers engage in predictable steps of the writing process—prewriting, drafting, revising, editing, publishing—they vary in how to begin, the order of the steps, the amount of time spent on each, and whether they need to return to certain steps mid-writing. In fact, an individual writer varies her writing process from piece to piece. This variation among students, and for students across pieces, is precisely what makes a workshop environment, which allows for individualization, so useful for writing instruction.

In 1983, Graves published *Writing: Teachers & Children at Work*, a groundbreaking book. Graves emphasizes craft from the start: "A craft is a process of shaping material toward an end. There is a long, painstaking, patient process demanded to learn how to shape material to a level where it is satisfying to the person doing the crafting" (p. 6). With Graves, learning to write is aligned with learning other crafts: by *doing* it all, one *learns* it all. The separate tasks involved in writing are put back together, and writers are taught the whole process—complex, nonlinear, multilayered, and driven by the unique writer—from the word go.

Literacy luminaries such as Lucy Calkins, Ralph Fletcher, JoAnn Portalupi, Georgia Heard, Shelley Harwayne, Carl Anderson, and Nancie Atwell walked through the door Graves had opened and refined this new approach to teaching writing. Calkins worked directly with Graves on his research into how writing develops in young children and, with that foundation, helped clarify the writing workshop method and introduce it to schools. The writing workshop became a place for children to express themselves, make choices, and learn craft. By the end of the 1990s, Harwayne (2000) even referred to writing workshop as "traditional" (p. 47). The writing workshop model was set to define writing instruction in the new century.

Writing workshop as we know it today is composed of a handful of core routines. Students carry notebooks to capture observations, funny moments, ideas, pictures, concerns, emotions, surprises, and wonderings, ideally throughout the school day and into their worlds outside of school. Genres are introduced and topics are suggested, but students have the choice to pursue what moves them—they write what their energy and interests direct them to write. Mentor texts are available in abundance. Mini-lessons directly explain writerly issues, such as where to get ideas for writing, appropriate responses to peers' pieces, using descriptive words, and how to include and punctuate dialogue. These lessons eschew the lecture format and are kept short in order to focus on one teaching point and maximize writing time. Furthermore, mini-lessons are often designed in response to the specific needs of the class and the questions or insights that have emerged during writing time. Conferences offer boundless opportunities between teacher and student to discuss, expand, deepen, answer, reinforce, and plan next steps. Whole-class shares—writing pieces, process anecdotes, or lessons learned— round out the workshop approach. Importantly, order and predictability help students navigate the workshop's openness and multiple resources. Experts on the workshop model fill a steady stream of books with discussions of these critical characteristics.

As an elementary-school teacher, I ate up writing workshop texts. I needed Calkins, Harwayne, and Fletcher after graduating from college, when I started working at a progressive downtown school in Manhattan. After all, I had not majored in education, as many of you likely are doing. It was not even an option at my small liberal arts school in Connecticut. I majored in sociology and carved a path through the program by focusing on social justice, social movements, stereotypes and assumptions about gender and sexuality, and power. I studied the sociology of education and subsequently wrote my 200-page thesis on power in schools. I learned about different types of power and investigated how administrators, teachers, students, and parents utilized their power to reach desired goals.

Early on, my students' classroom was also *my* classroom. My colleagues were my mentors, experienced and innovative and generous. My curriculum was, in large part, the spate of literacy books that showed me how the workshop approach to teaching writing is not only more effective, it is also far more enjoyable. And I learned from these books that my sociology background could still inform my teaching of writing. I believe literacy is the pathway to social justice, the most effective social movements are those that capitalize on story, identity affects the way we perceive the world and, in turn, make meaning for others, and power is a fluid resource that can be redistributed. I read in texts on writing workshop that power in the workshop, rather than held solely by a front-of-room instructor, is distributed among all the participants. Fletcher and Portalupi (2001) note, "Writing workshop turns the table and puts kids in charge" (p. 2). My eyes were opened; the foundation for my workshop was poured.

At the second school where I taught, an independent school for boys in New York, my colleague Katie Egan Cunningham and I inherited a traditional writing program, full of workbooks, quizzes, and fill-in-the-blank reports. When drafting informational texts on a U.S. state of their choosing, for example, the 40-plus students in our two rooms all led with the same sentence: "For my report, I researched the state of _____." Writing wasn't really writing. It wasn't even reminiscent of the writing process. It was plugging factors into a pre-determined formula.

The writing curriculum bothered me. It didn't match the writing workshop texts I had read. Plus, outside my classroom, I was a writer. In my home workshop—with its laptop, sticky notes, gel pens, paper clips, foam core boards, push pins, quotes, mentor texts, objects collected on trips, piano, guitar, and writer's notebook—I built essays, outlined books for children, and wrote songs that I performed in venues around the city. Nothing I crafted fit into a shell.

With the support of our administrator, Katie and I converted our writing block into a workshop. We compelled our boys to help create the environment in which they wanted to learn. We listened to their interests and responded by offering them the choice to pursue those interests in writing. We likened genres to tools, teaching our students that to accomplish a certain job (say, convincing your parents to buy you a pet fish), you must select the right tool (persuasive writing). Thus we firmly linked what our students were doing as writers with what they were doing in art class upstairs and shop class three floors down. We introduced a wealth of materials with which to build stories. We modeled how to provide meaningful feedback and emphasized how constructive comments help keep a piece's structure sound, which made both givers and receivers of that feedback feel comfortable and safe. And to those required state reports, we added one particularly shop-like piece; we had our students build three-dimensional floats to represent their states. Our second graders came alive. They cut, taped, glued, assembled, painted, strung, signed, and labeled. They carried their floats through the hallways on parade.

Just as Katie and I related writing to shop, I saw references to shops in iconic texts on writing. Authors discuss craft and technique, tools and materials, construction, design, and noise. Marilyn Pryle (2013) writes that on day one, she says to her middle-school students, "Think of this writing workshop as a woodworking class—all the tools are in this classroom, and you come here and use them to create" (p. 77). Katie Wood Ray (2001) envisions a workshop where, "It's a little noisy in the room, but it doesn't seem like a misdirected, off-task kind of noise. Just the hum of noise you get when people are working alongside one another" (p. 1). Ralph Fletcher and JoAnn Portalupi (2001) begin their workshop guide with a nod to shops of old, where "apprentices learned the skills of their trade by working at the sides of master craftsmen and women" (pp. 2–3). Lucy Calkins (1986) names a chapter on the connections between reading and writing, "Apprenticeships in the Writing Workshop: Learning from Authors" (p. 273).

Professional writers make similar references to shop. Celebrated *New Yorker* writer and memoirist Ian Frazier (Zinsser, 1998), for example, explains how he filled in his extraordinarily detailed nonfiction texts *Family* and *Great Plains* by using the language of carpentry: "It's like building a house. You get to a certain part and you realize you need a different gauge lumber or something, and you have to go get it" (p. 171). Fiction writer David Jauss (2008) also equates the challenge of building a collection of stories to the challenge of building a house: "We've got a pile of stories, all different sizes, shapes, textures, and colorations, and we have to find a way to assemble them that's both functional and aesthetically pleasing" (p. 152).

Author Michael Martone (2012) runs writing workshops for students in college and master's programs. He characterizes his workshops as "hypoxic," or "breathless," because his students must learn to write constantly in order to build endurance and strength. "Writing should be as natural as breathing," writes Martone. He goes on to clarify that much of the time, writing *isn't* natural to students because they don't feel safe in the writing environment. Martone writes that too often students are taught to write "… in an environment that privileges judgment, improvement, and success in narrowly defined metrics or binary distinctions of good and bad." In other words, a writing workshop ought not be a place where students achieve success by completing uniform assignments free of errors. It ought to be a place where students create and practice, free of the fear their writing doesn't measure up.

Author Natalie Goldberg relates writing to running in the same way. Of both, she says, "You practice whether you want to or not. You don't wait around for inspiration" (p. 11).

Shop elements don't take center stage in books on writing workshop or curriculum descriptions, but they are an essential part of the workshop foundation. They support. They invite, tantalize, and wait to be featured as the main event.

I like to show photographs of different kinds of workshops to my literacy students before we discuss the nature of a writing workshop. A tiny ceramic studio, a crowded darkroom strung with drying prints, a two-story boat-building shop where several people are working on a hull. I ask them to brainstorm what they see, to guess what the shops might sound and smell like. Here are some of the responses:

purposeful	passionate	appropriate space
hands-on	personalized	social
energetic	organized	collaborative
progressive	varied materials	quiet

I love this list, because it derives directly from observing the workshops I love to visit. I also love this list because it could easily come from observing a writing shop in action.

Collaborative, energetic, and purposeful. Tinkering, building, assembling. Tools and noise. Apprentices and masters. Mechanics and craft. It's time to take these words literally, to "shop up" our writing workshops, to infuse them with elements of other arts and industrial workshops and guarantee them to be just as transformative for our students.

I researched and reached out to master craftspeople who run workshops of all kinds—carpentry, quilting, scenery, robotics, visual arts, architecture, cooking, and more. I read and re-read texts on the writing workshop model and attended talks by art and shop teachers. Through my conversations and visits, I distilled seven core elements common to shops:

The Seven Elements of Shop
1. Master
2. Mess
3. Sense Stimulation
4. Workspace Variety
5. Safety Procedures
6. Technical Skills
7. Craft Techniques

Figure 1.3. Shop elements

Walk into any workshop and, chances are, you'll observe these seven elements. Through this book, I hope to show you that these elements are key to effective writing instruction as well.

A writing workshop, even one that contains all the essential ingredients such as choice and ample time to write, even one that beautifully matches the vision of the founders of the process approach, is best executed if it doesn't forget its namesake: the shop, the atelier, the studio in the basement where goods, and good things, are made.

CHAPTER 2

BUILDING THE ARGUMENT

Teachers grapple with how best to explain the complex and mysterious process of writing. In fact, they grapple with how to teach writing at all. In my course on the fundamentals of teaching, students new to education tell me that writing is the subject that most intimidates them.

While some teachers are converting their writing instruction to the workshop model, perfecting their development of mini-lessons, practicing their conference openers, devising skills trackers, and more, others have not yet adopted the workshop approach. Research shows that much of school-based writing instruction remains focused on writing for the acquisition of subject-related knowledge and technical composition skills, rather than writing for communication with others and development of voice and identity (Bazerman, 2016, pp. 11–12).

Since communication with others and development of voice and identity are two principles of the writing workshop model, teachers who adopt the model will find their students using their writing to participate in society, build relationships with audiences, and define themselves. Surely that is enough reason to convert to a writing workshop!

Furthermore, teachers who are aware of the elements of *shop*, and who ensure these elements are woven into their writing classes, will find three additional advantages for developing writers:

1. Shop reinstates exploratory play as a central component of learning to write.
2. Shop invites all types of learners to write, including English language learners, students with special needs, and students who show reluctance toward writing.
3. Shop supports the development and practice of off-page skills.

We want students to write. More, we want them to *want* to write. To *enjoy* writing. To live a writing life. Of course we do. We want students to like their learning environment, to engage in different content and projects, and to grow. Without at least a minimum of interest, our students can't be school citizens open to learning.

© KONINKLIJKE BRILL NV, LEIDEN, 2019 | DOI:10.1163/9789004397880_002

Shop both democratizes writing and elevates it. Shop removes writing from those single-skill drills that allow only a fraction of students to access, never mind enjoy, the practice. Learning to write isn't as logical as those exercises would have students believe. We risk alienating students by forcing them into a routine that isn't just ill-fitting for them, it's ill-fitting for the task. At the same time, shop highlights the fluidity and complexity of writing, while allowing students to converse about how to be a writer and what makes good writing. Students in writing shop have the chance to become sophisticated writers, readers, and thinkers.

In shop, writers *want* to write, not just for teacher evaluation, but out of curiosity and a natural love of exploration. Writers in shop want to write in order to make things—tangible, original, permanent things. Writers in shop want to write for a sense of belonging. Writers in shop want to write not just alongside peers, but with peers. And in the end, writers who want to write are writers who want to get better at it, who want to compose with stronger skills and new techniques, who want to carve out on paper their growing sense of who they are and where they fit in this world.

So, before we dive into the seven elements of shop, let's look at the three reasons why those shop elements are essential to writing instruction.

PLAY

As in any good shop or shop book, we also take the occasional break for some ribaldry, which means irreverent behavior, which means fun. (Offerman, 2016, p. 1)

Nick Offerman is one of my favorite actors. I loved his work on the TV show *Parks & Recreation*. When his character, salty small-town bureaucrat Ron Swanson, built a canoe, I got the sense there was something authentic behind the scene. I looked online and found that Offerman is a life-long self-proclaimed "woodchuck" who, before becoming an actor, built sets. When he's not touring or filming, he runs a woodshop along with his father and brother, crafting all sorts of beautiful things, including tables, benches, paddles, canoes, even ukuleles. In his book *Good Clean Fun*, Offerman (2016) writes, "Tool skills have certainly helped me earn a living over the years, but much more importantly, they have opened me up to a way of living, often in collaboration with other tool users (a.k.a. 'artists'), that has never stopped paying me dividends" (p. 2). Like Offerman, every serious writer I know talks of writing as a way of living, of "the writing life" and being a "literary citizen" who shares craft techniques with the community of writers.

Though certainly grounded in procedure, craft is more than procedural work. Offerman says he feels lucky to spend time learning and making in a shop: "It's simply an organic good time" (p. 12).

For my fortieth birthday, my husband planned a surprise party with the central theme of writing. My family and friends brainstormed words they thought represented me and posted them on a word wall. One sister started a story in a leather-bound journal, and all the guests continued the story sentence by sentence, idea by idea. Another sister brought a game of Jenga and asked everyone to write on the sides of the blocks; now, when we play Jenga, it's an original game full of funny and heartwarming messages we pull out and read. My brother-in-law set up a photo booth loaded with costume pieces that evoked Hollywood's version of the literary life: scarves, berets, glasses, worn journals, feather pens, a pipe. My friends, many of them writers, loved it; something about donning the outfits transformed us into playful little kids, which was particularly welcome given the decade I was entering. We snapped photo after photo, wrote page after page, and had a lot of fun.

Writing can be fun. Writing *should* be fun. At heart, writing is about playing with language to make something meaningful that will connect the self with others. With all the parts of speech and the tools to put them together, we build unusual things, things that have never been read before and may never be read again. Like making up a playground game or building a town out of LEGO, we construct meaning as we go. Our writing workshops, therefore, should be considered lands of opportunity.

And yet, ask students about writing class. Ask them if they like writing. Far too many say that writing is no fun. Far too many will even say *I hate writing*. And far too many of them are right. Writing class is missing the fun.

Alison Gopnik (2017), psychology and philosophy professor, proclaims the essentialism of play in children's lives. On an episode of the podcast "Hidden Brain," Gopnik tells host Shankar Vedantam about an experiment in which an adult shows a child a multi-function toy. When the adult gives the child the toy without limits, the child explores it openly. When the adult shows the child only one function of the toy, the child replicates only that single function. "Children are very, very sensitive to quite subtle indicators that someone's being pedagogical," says Gopnik, "that someone's being a teacher." Children follow the teacher's lead, only pursuing what the teacher has demonstrated. Gopnik argues that children widen their play possibilities when given unscripted time. You could teach a lesson on the exclamation mark, for example, and follow it with a standardized worksheet that asks students to select the "correct" sentence-ending punctuation. Or you could show children an exclamation mark through mentor texts and film subtitles, on dry-erase boards in a multitude of colors, through a game of charades, on a block of wood that can be placed on the writing surface each time it is useful—and let them play.

Gopnik goes on to describe how unscripted play not only widens the range of activities, but also lifts the quality of activities. She explains, for example, how much better robots do on tasks when they are first given a period of play. They explore, learn the environment, dance around, figure out what they are capable of doing with their robot parts. "Then give it a specific job," says Gopnik. "The robot was more resilient if it had a chance to play." Gopnik also discusses how younger children learn best when given the opportunity to play, while older children learn best in an apprenticeship system after having grown through years of play. Play is the foundational learning mode; all else, including the master/apprentice model of the shop, follows naturally.

Educator Erika Christakis (2016) bridges play to formal education in *The Importance of Being Little*. She devotes a chapter of her book to criticism of the traditional cut-and-paste preschool project, claiming that such activities do a disservice to children. Those cut-and-paste crafts remind me of the fill-in-the-blank reports I inherited while teaching second grade. Christakis calls us to action: "It's time to question the continued hold of what I would call counterfeit crafts over our preschool curriculum" (p. 71). The ubiquitous hand-traced Thanksgiving turkey, for example, is inferior to real-world, hands-on experiences of autumn. Christakis suggests a corner devoted to play, one that can be filled with turkey-related items, like farm tools and animal food (p. 71). Christakis's ideas about arts in the preschool classroom are easily applied to a shop-like writing workshop:

> When the preschool classroom environment is carefully constructed to serve as the laboratory for learning, young children learn what we set out to teach them, but they also learn—and this is critical—the whole wealth of things we haven't set out to teach them explicitly. In today's world of expanding facts, this flexibility is essential. (p. 75)

Later, Christakis describes "pro-writing" classrooms, which are classrooms that incorporate writing materials into every corner and activity. Dramatic play, for example, includes not only costumes and real-life props, but writing utensils, paper, clipboards, and chalkboards. Children are taught to see writing "not so much as work that must be slogged through (before heading outside to recess) but as a source of joy in itself, a whirring conduit for meaning, content knowledge, and the expression of feelings, including affection and pride" (p. 236). A writing shop, like the preschool room Christakis describes, is a laboratory for learning. Through exploration and play, writers discover novel ways to put together words, punctuation, and empty space.

I know first-hand how essential is play. One of my sons, from birth, has developed atypically. Movement in particular, like rolling over or pulling to stand, has not come naturally to him. My husband and I have held his hand every step of the way—literally. Our diagnostic journey led to a rare genetic syndrome. Our geneticist told my husband and me that our son's syndrome has extreme variability in expression; some children with the syndrome grow up showing a number of life-changing symptoms, while others grow up showing no symptoms at all. We were alarmed at first, but the geneticist said to simply watch for speech. If our son started talking by three years old, we'd be gifted an open window into his inner world, and that would help us understand where he was developmentally. We were told to observe him at play and listen for sounds and words. Don't intervene, it was emphasized. *Just let him play.* My husband and I learned to let our son's play time unfold organically.

By three, my son's play grew as rich as we hoped it could be. He'd fix his car carrier's boo-boo with masking tape, then load it up with farm animals. "Be careful!" he'd tell the plastic animals while giving them a ride over to the play kitchen so all could watch his wooden pizza cooking, pretend birthday candles and all. "It's a pizza farm birthday party!"

Because of the syndrome, it is deeply engrained in me to allow leaps of logic and flights of imagination and take them as signs of a rich internal life. And because of the central loss of my own life, the loss of my father and childhood memory, I am keenly interested in watching my own children play. My son's funny connections at three years old were not signs of misunderstanding how the world works; rather, they were signs of a young brain assimilating everything it saw—character, setting, purpose, tools, boo-boos—and creating a world over which he had total control. Now, a few years later, his play worlds are even more complicated and imaginative. His mind and body at play are in full-on development mode. He is growing, he is learning, precisely because he is playing.

Educators and families share concerns about the lack of time to accomplish growing task lists, the reduction of recess, and the disappearance of exploratory play. A string of articles and books reveals our culture's pushback against the increasingly rigid classroom routines that leave little room for open play. Play is, after all, exactly the frame of mind that produces the most rewards. Shelley Harwayne (2000) connects play with the writing shop in this way:

It strikes me that children who have had lots of experiences designing, cutting, pasting, carving, sketching, painting, decorating, pretending, and otherwise messing around creatively take more readily to the process of writing. Children who know how to play seem to approach writing with the required openness it takes to craft quality work. These fortunate children seem more at ease playing around with words, ideas, images, formats, and the like. (p. 19)

While writing, students should play with words and ideas. They should develop worlds over which they have total control. And yes, in writing shop, they should design, cut, paste, carve, sketch, paint, decorate, pretend, and play around.

Recently, I attended an event at my children's public elementary school about "purposeful play," an initiative captured in a book by the same title by teachers Kristine Mraz, Alison Porcelli, and Cheryl Tyler (2016). Administrators and teachers at the school are studying purposeful play, which is play that enhances learning and builds skills, in order to incorporate play across the curriculum. At the event, parents and staff played together—tossing Frisbees into bins, building with blocks and tubes, even maneuvering through a game of Twister—and observed what happens while we do. The more playful the game, the more vulnerable we became, and the more laughter, bonding, and release that followed.

After play time, teachers shared stories from their classrooms about how play is a central component of classroom life. The art teacher described her classroom as a "shop" where she makes available all sorts of materials with which students can play.

The school principal, a few weeks later, explained the same play initiative to parents of incoming kindergarteners. She talked about the school's STEAM Lab, with its magnet wall and 3-D printer, where science, technology, engineering, art, and math are explored. The principal shared how some of the younger students turned plain white t-shirts into lab coats and strutted to the lab, ready to explore. Children *love* science, she observed, in a way they don't always love reading or writing. Of course, I was thinking, they can love writing too! Just imagine a writing shop that matches a STEAM Lab in excitement and invention.

My writing shops are always ripe with play opportunities. From word games to story starters, we play, and often find ourselves playing right into a new story or piece. When a student named Joaquim was stuck on how to describe what it felt like to be kicked in the shin, I brought him out to the hallway where we both tried kicking ourselves in the shin—it's not easy! When Genesis was recovering from an illness and showed little energy, we played a mystery word game until she re-engaged, then used the mystery word in a sentence. When Jeremy wanted to end every sentence with an exclamation mark, I asked him to read his piece and hop up each time he saw an exclamation mark. He was tired by the end, and we discussed how it's tiring for a reader to read all those exclamation marks too. Soon, Salvador, Alexander, and Nicole wanted to hop too. So we added raised shoulders for questions marks and folded arms for periods. Reading aloud became something of a rhythmic dance. Once, I came across a Mickey Mouse reading pointer and left it on a desk. Two boys used it to choose sentence starters with flare and build a story together.

Figure 2.1. Selecting sentence starters

We honor the open-ended nature of play by maintaining an open-ended shop atmosphere. I agree wholeheartedly with writing coach Colleen Cruz (2008), who asks,

> If a student rarely, if ever, gets a chance to daydream and wander and stumble onto a great idea, or else actively skim different strategy charts and harangue friends for ideas, when is the child ever going to learn how to cultivate that generative side of writing? (p. 55)

Students in shop will learn to generate writing, often in that "hypoxic" way prioritized by teacher-writer Michael Martone.

I ask my education students this question: when you think of a professional author, what kind of person do you picture in your mind? Why not ask children the same and borrow those presumed styles for dressing in the shop? Why not allow students to stuff their arms into different clothes and hang something special from their necks, like those t-shirt lab coats, and see what happens? And why not, as writing teachers, don something new for workshop? Why not model for students what play looks and feels like? Is there anything more exciting to students than watching their own teacher engaged in play? Play to shift your students' state of mind and point of view.

When I first made the turn from grade-school teacher to writer and writing teacher, I attended a summer conference for writers run by a literary magazine in Ohio. Author and writing instructor Rebecca McClanahan (2001) was my workshop leader, and she designed a space in which we students could use in our work whatever the world introduced—a raging thunderstorm, hot dorm rooms, new friendships. In her writing craft book, while describing personal writing, McClanahan says,

> Thinking of writing as a playroom rather than a workroom is one of the many ways to discover, or rediscover, the joy of private writing. A playroom has no boundaries. Now it's a submarine taking you under. Now it's a forest, dark and unexplored, where exotic creatures lurk. Now it's a trunk filled with dress-up clothes. Now it's the door to an unwritten story for which you have the only key, and, wonder of wonders, the key fits. (p. 40)

Similarly, Natalie Goldberg (1986) says of writing, "It's a place that you can come to wild and unbridled, mixing the dream of your grandmother's soup with the astounding clouds outside your window" (p. 13).

Both McClanahan and Goldberg equate writing space with play space, where different materials and participants, often seemingly in contrast to each other, bring about something entirely new. I for one want to spend time in that place of play, the place where I can have some good clean fun. And I want my students to go there too.

INCLUSION

Kids enjoy classes like shop, gym, and band because there's a premium on *doing* the activity rather than talking about it. (Fletcher & Portalupi, 2001, p. 2)

After my father left the Navy, he worked at a power plant, enrolled in a master's program, and, in his free time, played in his basement workshop. When he died, my mother set up a scholarship foundation in his name. Our annual scholarship awards funds to a high-school senior for post-high-school education. Critical to my mother and my parents' friends, who served on the board of directors when the scholarship was first established, was that high-school students enrolling in vocational school or taking classes in technical fields would be eligible for the award. After all, many of my parents' family members and friends did just that; rather than attend college, they learned a trade and became masters of craft. For us, it didn't matter whether a student hopped on the four-year college track, the way it did to many of the scholarship organizers at the time. Our foundation wanted all students to have the chance to grow in their chosen area. I've never forgotten that early lesson on inclusion.

Shop is, by nature, inclusive. It's a place to build stuff. To fix broken things, to make things whole again. At its heart, shop invites every participant to enter its door and mess around with its materials. No fingers are told, *don't touch.* No body is told, *sit still.* No mind is told *don't think differently, don't connect, don't create.* And in shop, when things fall apart, the building materials are still there, piled on the workbench, waiting for a new iteration. Natalie Goldberg (1986) says writers should not set out to write a particular piece. Rather, writers should feel free "to write the worst junk in the world" (p. 11). You can always come back to the junk pile. You can always tinker.

Research shows that English language learners benefit from a writing environment that develops "metalanguage to talk and think about their writing for school tasks" (Cumming, 2016, p. 366). ELLs do better as writers when they can talk about their writing freely, interact with peers over writing, share their writing, and use author language to describe their writing. The immersion in writing, as opposed to the more simplistic procedure of direct instruction/related worksheet, is what helps ELLs grow as writers. Collaborative writing activities, like those available in a writing shop, "have

19

been shown to provide contexts for language students to support one another, articulate their ideas with, and learn language from their peers" (Cumming, 2016, p. 366).

Additionally, because of its flexibility, and because it privileges variety, shop allows students to bring their home languages to their craft. I had a fourth grader named Jefferson who was growing up in a Spanish-speaking household. While he spoke fluent English, he often switched to Spanish during shop, especially when exclaiming surprise, delight, or frustration. One day, Jefferson was writing a true story and wanted to record what his father said to him during a heated moment, but he struggled to translate his father's words into English. We could have worked on the translation, though my Spanish is too limited to be of real help. Instead, I showed him that incorporating both Spanish and English—code-switching—is a sophisticated technique that can make a narrative realistic and dynamic to read. Many children's book authors (e.g., Sandra Cisneros) and writers for adults (e.g., Gloria Anzaldúa) use code-switching. Our shop created the opportunity for this exchange to occur. Jefferson felt safe, had choice, trusted me, took a risk, and happened upon a writing technique that I did not predict and plan for in a mini-lesson. Other students nearby immediately wanted to incorporate words and phrases in their native languages or in languages they were learning at the time.

Many of my students have inserted native language into their writing. One third grader, Emely, on her very first day of shop, was listing what good writers do, and chose to begin with: "Eyos ban al libor a escibe." We needed to dig through two layers of meaning: one, spelling in Spanish, then two, translating to English. *They go to the book to write.* I doubt the translation is accurate, but I can't get that lovely line out of my head. "The book"— whether our own book in progress, a friend's book, a mentor book—speaks to something greater than ourselves as individual writers. Sometimes when I sit to work, the line returns to my head: *I go to the book to write.*

Educator Valerie Kinloch (2012) conducted a study over the course of a year with culturally and linguistically diverse (CLD) students attending an urban high school. Her students were reluctant to see themselves as writers, "particularly in comparison to their white peers" (Kinloch & Burkhard, p. 378). In time, however, the students developed a new definition of "writer" and learned how external forces, not internal ones, cast them as non-writers (p. 388). Kinloch's writing shop,

> … invited students to co-design writing assignments, engage in small
> and whole-group writing and reading discussions, utilize popular culture

and other familiar cultural referents in their writings, and determine ways to align their writing assignments with larger learning goals that they came to name for themselves. (p. 388)

The emphasis on building in shop, as opposed to the input/output procedure in traditional writing classrooms, is at the heart of stronger writing instruction. Rather than leave behind their identities, English language learners and CLD students maintain their identities while writing in shop.

I find myself increasingly anxious about how my son, with a syndrome that makes fine-motor tasks quite challenging, will "fit" into his writing classroom. One of the many reasons my husband and I moved to our current town is for its strong, progressive schools. Children are introduced to writing workshop in kindergarten. As a mother of a young student with special needs, therefore, I am particularly moved by the story of Nancy Shelton, an upper-elementary teacher at a high-needs school, who was asked to include nine students with various disabilities in her classroom of typically developing students for a year. While the rest of her school focused on direct teaching of language and grammar, Shelton chose the writing workshop model, specifically so that she could include her students with disabilities. She paid special attention to some of the shop elements I describe in this book. For example, to emphasize the safety procedures common to all shops, Shelton "settled on community building as her first task when the school year started" (Fu & Shelton, 2007, p. 333). To ensure workspace variety, she allowed her students to move around the room, work solo on the floor, team up with a partner, or join a group at a table. To underscore the need for a master writer, she claimed that role for herself until she noticed certain students learning from their peers; gently, she transferred the master/apprentice relationship to the students. In order to serve students with special needs, Shelton not only created a writing workshop in a school that had never had one before, she tuned into the very elements that make a workshop a shop at all, and saw plenty of evidence of success as a result.

Many—too many—students regard themselves as non-writers, or bad writers. Some educators classify these students as "struggling," but I prefer to use the word "reluctant." I've never had a reluctant writer who stayed reluctant the entirety of writing workshop. There are so many materials to choose from, so many places to work, so many ways to wake up the senses, so many mentor texts available, that even the most reluctant writers find their way to the page. Even if it takes a while.

Johnny, one of my second graders and a reluctant reader and writer, finally clicked with my literacy curriculum when I used *How Are You Peeling?* by Saxton Freymann and Joost Elffers (2004) as a mentor text. After sharing the book, which contains images of fruits and vegetables carefully sculpted to evoke human emotions, I asked the students to respond in a way that meant something to them. Many students drew pictures of food and wrote short lines to accompany them. Some stretched to find new feelings-based adjectives to illustrate. But Johnny did not write; rather, at home that evening, he carved a happy face into a lemon. His instinct was to *make*, to participate in a surprising way. He took a big risk. And when he showed me his lemon the next day, he beamed, bright as his creation. I accepted his contribution with something near reverence. From that day, Johnny's confidence as a writer seemed more robust. He willingly came to workshop, knowing he had made something unique and important.

One day, a fourth grader named Felix, despite being surrounded by students humming along in shop, refused to write anything. He visited the bathroom, then the water fountain, then the bathroom again. I asked why he felt reluctant to write that day. He was tired, he said. Tired from the day. "And I don't want to be here." It's OK to write about being tired, I said. To write about not wanting to be here in writing shop. He looked at me skeptically as the power difference between us leveled out. And then he wrote a four-line poem about not wanting to be in writing shop. He chose that piece to be published in our shop book (see Figure 2.2).

I recall a story Donald Graves (1983) tells in his seminal book on how students learn to write. A teacher named Mr. Bangs was determined to convert his writing classroom, which had been "a tight ship," to a workshop (p. 33). At first, it was an exercise in patience: the students were disorganized and constantly interrupting conferences. Three students, Fred, Albert, and Tom, "started pestering neighbors, making much more noise than ordinary" (p. 34). Mr. Bangs evaluated what was happening with the three boys. Turns out, they were "afraid to write, had major problems in handwriting and spelling, didn't like the appearance of their work, and hadn't yet found a territory of interest" (p. 36). Mr. Bangs overhauled the workspace of the room, assigning places for everything. He invited his students to become apprentices, meeting with them often at first until they found topics of interest. He offered them "increased access to each other," not decreased, in order to help them learn how to help each other (p. 37). And as time went on, all the children, even the reluctant ones, "had a place and a purpose in the total fabric of the room" (p. 39).

No Fun!

I am mad cause I had no fun no gym no energy worst day!
I hate here no fun always writing why!
I wish I was not here.
I wish I was home.

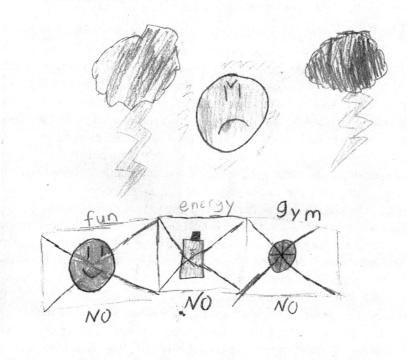

Figure 2.2. No Fun!, by Felix, grade 3

Students can't write if they don't feel welcome at the table. Students can't write if they feel anxious or boxed in. Students must feel safe and trusting if they are to clear the path from internal idea to external writing. In a writing shop, students of all backgrounds and skill levels, students like Johnny, Jefferson, Felix, and my own son, can find a way in. Because in shop, the act of writing is like the act of making anything else. We can all make things in shop.

OFF-PAGE SKILLS

> These fine parents taught my sisters and me moral courage, insofar as we have it, and tolerance, and how to dance all night without dragging your arms on your partner, and how to time the telling of a joke. (Dillard, 1998, p. 151)

In my first graduate school program, I took a course on novel writing. Little did I know when I signed up, the course would be a writing shop. Under the gentle mentorship of our instructor, my classmates and I built a novel from scratch, which involved character sketches, narrative development, sharing time, discussion, and field trips. Duos and trios met up outside class to try different writing methods. Someone I met in that class remains one of my closest friends. Our characters seemed to be ready to meet in the story, so we met in person, writing back and forth on the same laptop, dialoguing aloud and then translating that to the page. We still reference our characters as if they are living relatives that frustrate and charm us.

The novel course was an exercise in collaboration. With ten voices fighting to be heard, and with the goal of writing one cohesive piece by the end, we learned quickly how to negotiate, insert ourselves, and let go. When one student ran ahead in prose with another student's character, tactfulness became paramount. When one character released an unexpected diatribe against the others, conflict arose among the writers. We worked to separate the writer's disposition from his character's and figured out how to compromise with each other without compromising our dignity and right to free speech. Our collaboration could not be measured, nor could it be considered individually. Sure, we grew stronger as writers, leaving the semester with more skills and some new techniques, all of which could be measured. Yet, collaboration was the *primary* goal of the course. Without acquiring and using the off-page skills of tact, compromise, and reading the room, to name a few, our community would have failed the course. We would not have created the multi-character novel that was asked of us.

Researcher Peter Johnston (2012) names collaboration as not only critical to education, but critical to humanity. He writes, "Our main advantage as human beings lies in our ability to think together" (p. 93). Yet thinking together is still subsumed under individual achievement in schools. Johnston adds, "We continue to view children solely in terms of their individual academic development and the individual cognitive processes they will need to succeed on individual tests" (pp. 93–94). Johnston's work, which builds on work by a host of others, emphasizes skills outside the traditional ones listed in workbooks and included in standards.

All these skills—collaboration, flexibility, tactfulness, conflict resolution—are what I call off-page skills, skills that can be introduced, developed, and observed, but not measured on the page. Nowhere are these skills better reinforced than in a shop setting. As Fletcher and Portalupi (2001) point out, teaching writing involves helping children gain a number of on-page skills like sequencing and supporting ideas. Teaching writing in a workshop environment also "creates an environment where students can acquire these skills, along with the fluency, confidence, and desire to see themselves as writers" (p. 1). Teacher Kyle Schwartz (2016) also notes the importance of these off-page skills, writing, "As educators, when we start recognizing things like joy, energy, and curiosity as resources and visible skills, we can leverage them in our classrooms" (p. 54).

My friend Danielle is an artist who creates watercolor images and transfers them to wallpaper, towels, stationery, and more. When I asked her what she focuses on when she teaches others her craft, she said without hesitation, "confidence." An elusive skill: being certain of your worth, your achievements, and whatever it is you have to offer. With certainty comes self-reliance. Danielle tells me that in her visual art shop, "confidence matters over every other thing" (D. Wolf, personal communication, January 6, 2017).

Whenever I think about off-page skills and writing, I'm reminded of a story by writer Barbara Feinberg (2011) that I like to share with my students. Director of a creative arts program for children, Feinberg describes the moment her nine-year-old daughter shared a sentence from a story she'd written, a sentence she was gobsmacked at having crafted all by herself: "What could they do; there was nothing to be done" (p. 30). Feinberg explores her reaction to that sentence, which grew from dismissal, to recognition, to awe of her daughter's discovery: "[T]he fact that she remained so surprised by her sentence suggested that its invention had occurred not through careful planning, or conscious design, but through a kind of dreamy intuition" (p. 31). It is this dreamy intuition that the writing shop grants. There's the play, there's the inclusion. And there's something else too. For Feinberg's daughter, creating a beautiful sentence took courage, confidence, and a sixth sense to know the sentence was something different, something lovely. The sentence sprang from adventure. "She seemed to regard her having written it as one who finds herself plunked down in the middle of somewhere she'd half set out to find, but having arrived, is not at all sure how she'd gotten there," writes Feinberg. "I was an adult sitting with a child in the mysteries of the creative realm" (p. 31).

Three of my students, Valeria, Eliot, and Alex, were goofing off during writing workshop one afternoon. I sensed Valeria might like to be writing, but the two boys sitting nearby would have preferred to be outside playing soccer. (It was a beautiful spring day!) I dug out of the closet a few hand-held dry-erase boards and markers and left them on the table for the trio to explore. Drawn to the new materials, the students began chatting about them, practicing writing with different colors. Soon, they were collaborating on a story. Valeria took the lead, constructing sentences and leaving blanks for details, while Eliot and Alex happily provided nouns and verbs, like a team Madlibs game. The story spilled over onto the next board and the next, until they asked me for more. I took photos of the boards so they could erase and keep going without losing what had already been written.

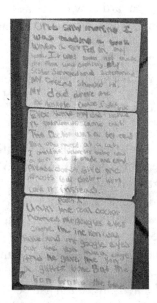

Figure 2.3. Collaborative writing by students in grade 4

Not only did the students develop a new fictional story, and not only did they overcome a hurdle of starting, and not only did they grow a little stamina for writing that day, they developed a new camaraderie with social roles to play. Next writing workshop, they wanted to sit with each other again.

Numerous skills beyond the technical skills of writing are at play in shop. Self-awareness, impulse control, seeking help, listening carefully, cooperation, conflict negotiation, appropriate risk-taking, grit, initiative, courage, consideration of the health and well-being of others: all are taught and reinforced particularly well in a shop setting. In fact, shop, with its mess and sense stimulation, with its variety of workspaces and safety procedures, necessitates the development of such off-page skills. Emphasizing these skills can have an extraordinarily positive effect on students' views toward learning how to write.

CAPTAIN OF THE SHOP

Master

That's the way it is with craft, whether it be teaching or writing. There is a road, a journey to travel, and there is someone to travel with us, someone who has already made the trip. (Graves, 1983, p. 6)

I waited in a shop full of wood. The room smelled fresh and piney. Unsanded pieces in progress looked impressive just as they were, but I imagined the splinters that threatened gloveless fingers. Minuscule flecks of sawdust floated in the light from the fluorescent ceiling bulb. By the door, aprons hung on hooks. Vehicles, some detailed and some still roughly hewn, lay on tables. A boy, nine or ten, leaned over a workbench a few feet away, wearing a white apron that protected his button-down shirt and corduroy pants. He was attaching a rubber band to his model of a catapult. The quiet work was overlaid by the gentle voice of the shop teacher, who showed the student just how to pull the band taut. The boy stood uncommonly still as he watched a master at work.

The boy's teacher, Gary, glanced my way and put up a finger: he'd be with me in a minute. I was a second-grade teacher upstairs, where my classroom was now locked up after a long but productive day. My basement visit shifted me from teacher to student, mentor to apprentice, because Gary was teaching me to play the guitar. Until then, I'd been writing songs but could not accompany myself. Gary is a skilled guitarist, but it was his passion for music, and also for teaching, that drew me down to the basement. He was not a demonstrative person, but I knew he wanted me to love the music I produced with my own hands. To me, Gary was a master guitarist, just as to his young student, he was a master craftsman. I loved descending to the basement once a week to sit among the workbenches, tools, safety equipment, and student creations. There was so much potential in the room, which made me feel a little more confident. Learning to play guitar surrounded by the evidence of hands-on craftsmanship, particularly the pieces in progress that had not yet been perfected, was invigorating.

© KONINKLIJKE BRILL NV, LEIDEN, 2019 | DOI:10.1163/9789004397880_003

Each shop teacher is both master and mentor: master in relation to the craft at hand, and mentor in relation to the apprentice learning the craft. The master/apprentice relationship is as old as humanity. With the dawn of settled societies came the need to teach craft and trade so that knowledge would not die out. Now, we can take classes in almost anything. We can start down the path to mastery of cheese making, beer brewing, locksmithing, needlepointing, woodcarving, seamanship, spirituality, even Jedi training, which my 11-year-old nephew considers his destiny. But, as Nick Offerman (2016) points out, we still need a master. "[L]earning any physical discipline," he writes, "will always be much easier to achieve under the in-person guidance of someone who has been down the road before you" (p. 86).

My sister Beth, once an apprentice to my mother in her seamstress shop, is now a master quilter. In her basement studio, the garage she and her husband converted into her workshop, Beth's three children, their friends and classmates, and children and adults from her town gather to learn how to sew together fabrics and apply designs. She creates round-robin projects, for which she and her apprentices all add elements.

Figure 3.1. Beth, master quilter, guides Nina, grade 4

My friend Eric is another master of craft. A theater technician with training in automation, museum display, and college theater, Eric once ran a summer theater program for young students. His former position as a scene shop foreman with the Royal Shakespeare Company made him uniquely qualified to lead his students of all ages from sketch to stage, as they learned how to drill, hammer, and paint along the way. Eric happens to be quite tall, and I love that his younger students literally looked up—way, way up—to him.

As I write, I just dropped my eldest son off for his first day of farm camp. He loves to water our garden, trim our grape vine, deadhead our flowers, and tend our tiny vegetable patch. So a week at farm camp was the perfect way for him to begin the summer. He noted the difference from the school setting right away—outside, in the sunshine, surrounded by the smells of woodchips and goats and grass—and stood excitedly in front of the "apprentice garden" for a picture. Soon, his counselor, Pam, led him to the berry patch to begin the morning.

Without Beth, Eric, Gary, and Pam to show, cajole, reinforce, suggest, spark, and navigate, the shop, though wonderfully exciting at first, could quickly overwhelm or bore young students. They need guides to feel less like short-term visitors in unfamiliar places and more like long-term apprentices who can, one day, fill their masters' shoes.

We are tasked to be the master craftspeople in our writing shops, too. Our students look to us for knowledge, experience, and advice. Each time I teach a class on writing workshop, I ask the teacher candidates to generate a list of essentials for what makes an effective writing teacher. Without fail, each group lists as number one: *passion about writing*. We need not be professional writers; we must, however, be passionate about what writing is and what it can do, passionate about the books we read to our students, passionate about the works of art they in turn create. We must hold up published texts and revere them, pointing out all the ways professional authors are skilled and use different techniques to make the stories come alive. After all, how can new writers invest in writing if the master is not invested?

Further, we must write. Let me repeat that: *we must write*. As Donald Graves (1983) says, "We don't find many teachers of oil painting, piano, ceramics, or drama who are not practitioners in their field. Their students see them in action in the studio" (p. 6).

Yet, when it comes to the writing shop, many teachers tell me they could not possibly be masters. They don't consider themselves to be strong enough writers. Some grab at seed ideas and try drafting a little over the summers or holidays, but often let these ideas sit when the incredibly busy school year starts unfolding. When they do write, it's most often to record observations of their students, log incidents, provide feedback on student work, or write notes to send home by backpack mail. Most claim the only writing they do outside of work is over text and email. Teachers fear teaching writing when they don't self-identify as good writers, especially when it comes to the very content they ask their students to write: essays, stories, letters, poems.

I'm not immune to similar feelings of inadequacy. Since I work in both writing and education, I find myself splitting my time and energy between both, while writing friends leap ahead. They read much more than I do, write much more than I can, and pursue success in all its forms: publications, grants, fellowships, residencies, and more. I spend a large percentage of my work time planning, teaching, reading drafts and offering feedback, and grading, rather than writing. Plus, as a parent of young children, I am constantly attending to their needs, rather than writing *or* teaching. Have I mastered writing? Teaching? Parenting? Hardly.

And so, when I stand before a class of education students, I must remind them (and myself) that I am a working writer in addition to being their teacher. Even if I've spent just one hour writing that week, I say this: I have spent time writing this week, and so have you. I have mastered elements of writing, and so have you. In relation to our students, *we are already masters*. We perform the master role. We may in fact be the very first "professional" authors our students have ever known. It's true that in the publishing industry, most teachers don't have books, stories, and poems out there (though a number of them do). But to our students, we write weekly newsletters, headline classroom blogs, and write sample stories for our mini-lessons. We write to our students and their families. We select mentor texts from the library and read with gusto. We are, therefore, mastering the craft in front of their eyes.

Luckily for us, writing workshop makes investment in writing much easier, for us as well as for our students. We are as positively affected by the shop environment as our students are. Along with our students, we can dive into workshop and come up with something novel, perhaps even a story that may be the next seed idea. We write alongside our students. We discover as they discover. By stepping outside prescribed workbooks, we mix up tools and materials for our students and use those tools and materials ourselves. Our innate and perhaps long-hidden instinct to play can be aroused in a writing shop the way it is in an art studio.

Author Frank McCourt (1998) describes teaching at Stuyvesant High School in Manhattan as the experience that made him less a traditional schoolteacher and more "human" (p. 75). His immersion as a mentor in writing workshop helped him write his Pulitzer-Prize-winning memoir, *Angela's Ashes*. Of those teaching years, McCourt says, "That's where I learned to drop the mask. … Whatever I did in that classroom spilled over into the book" (p. 76). I am living through the same phenomenon right now. What I do with my students is spilling over onto this page.

One Wednesday afternoon, an eight-year-old named Anthony crossed his arms over his paper, pen inert, eyes fixed on some distant spot. I sat next to him, turned over a loose worksheet, and began writing on the blank side. Glancing up, I noticed Anthony was watching me, so I looked around the room and began to talk writer talk. "I want to write about something unexpected happening. I'm looking at that giant fan, and that giant American flag, and I'm thinking, what would happen if the flag suddenly got sucked into the fan?" Anthony looked from flag to fan and, without me asking him to, responded: "All the cloth parts would get destroyed, but the metal parts would be ok." I told him, "I'm stuck on that part. Do you think you could write the next sentence of the story?" And he did. And the next one, and the next. It was a risk for us both. It was playful. It was a one-on-one, very human interaction about the work of writing. It was as simple as this: I wrote, he wrote.

A few weeks later, one of my graduate students tried the same exercise with third-grader Joel. She wrote, he wrote: the most fundamental way to guide a student (see Figure 3.2).

In the writing shop, teachers, simply by writing in front of their students, writing with their students, and initiating writer talk, are performing the role of master craftsperson. As celebrated writer, professor, and writing coach, Donald Murray (1985) describes, when you converse with a student about his writing, you are engaging in "the working talk of fellow writers sharing their experience with the writing process" (p. 120).

Critically, the master writer in a shop knows when to step back and allow students to explore on their own. When I first started teaching, this particular skill did not come naturally to me. In fact, it still doesn't. I often have to consciously pull away from student writing, not because I'm tempted to correct it, but because I am tempted to engage deeply with it. Sometimes, though, engagement with a master will derail the apprentice. So I let Hans write that his perfect sandwich would include gas and chalk, and I let William design a sport about hunting for a plastic wolf. I didn't intervene when Edgar wrote about a soccer player sustaining an "ingery" or when the nature of the rats in Samanta's story swung illogically between meanness and kindness. Blake opened his story with "My bobsled is red and I once led the way" and while it did cross my mind that I could ask him to split those two thoughts, save the second one for later, I couldn't stop thinking of how perfectly it opened his piece. How lyrical, how rhythmic, like a poem.

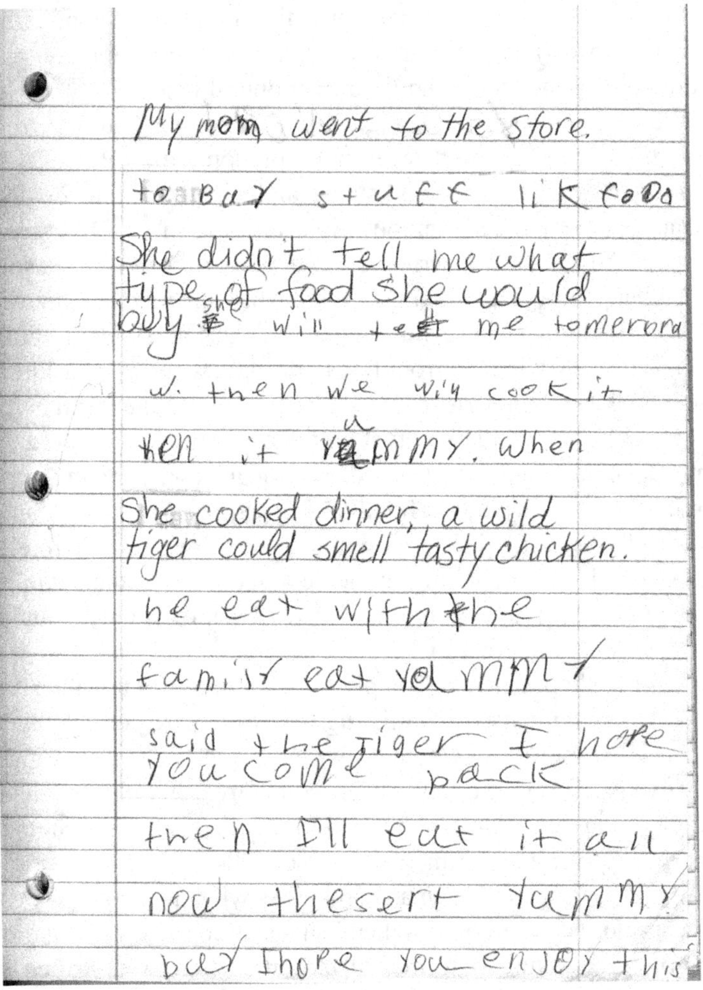

My mom went to the store.
to Buy stuff liK food
She didn't tell me what
type of food she would
buy will tell me tomerora
w. then we will cook it
then it yummy. When
She cooked dinner, a wild
tiger could smell tasty chicken.
he eat with the
family eat yo mmy
said the tiger I hope
you come back
then I'll eat it all
now thesert tammy
buy I hope you enjoy this

Figure 3.2. Collaborative writing between teacher and student

As students become masters of their craft, they simultaneously master specific pieces of the workshop routine. There is almost nothing more powerful a boost to students' confidence than allowing them to share what they are best at doing. Kleydi is really good at adding details. Valeria can lead the way on collaborative writing. Manuel is a master of the David collection by David Shannon—he knows all the books inside and out. Let other students apprentice themselves. Go to Kleydi for help adding details. Go to Valeria if you want to collaborate on a piece. Go to Manuel if you want to use a David book as a mentor text and write about being naughty. Because of the shop's reinforcement of the master/apprentice relationship and the leveling out of power, students are nearly as likely to step into the master role as their teachers are.

My father's best friend in the Navy was a fellow submariner named Bob. He and his wife stayed very close with my family after my father died. After 26 years in the Navy, with two submarine commands behind him, Bob retired from the service and became a physics and chemistry teacher. He says he knew, while still serving, that he had to be a teacher, that he hoped his classroom would feel as inspiring as his submarines did. He admits he didn't have teaching experience going in. But he had passion. He wanted to show his students that scientists and engineers are influential people. At his school, Bob founded a robotics workshop, where one of my favorite photos of him was taken: a teenaged boy stands at a workbench covered with batteries and wires. He points to the needle on a voltage meter that's connected by several alligator clips to the batteries. His mentor, Bob, looks on, a smile on his face as he likely knows the student will be getting the data he needs. *We have power!*

Fifteen years after leaving the Navy, Bob's former submariners and students still call him "the captain."

Teachers who write, and writers who teach, can make the same impression, can be looked at by their current and former students as the captain, the guide, the master.

NUTS AND BOLTS

Mess

It's a privilege to muck about in sentences all morning. (Dillard, 1998, p. 160)

My eldest sister, Beth, the professional quilter, crafts everything from wedding quilts to name signs for newborns sewn from bright, adorable fabric. Beth and her husband converted their two-car garage into her quilting studio. They did the work themselves, creating a space designed exactly with her needs in mind. They live in southeast Massachusetts, so the weather isn't always warm. Beth is constantly on the lookout for warm slipper-like shoes that still provide lots of support for the long hours she's standing at her workbench.

Beth's workshop is all shape and color. Her bolts of fabric seem immeasurable. Thick and thin textiles in solid colors. Cotton, canvas, and jersey. Kelly green with purple elephants, royal blue with ribbons, petal pink with cupcakes. Stripes, solids, squiggles, paisleys, polka dots, and plaids. There's thread, backing, and buttons. Tools overwhelm the flat surfaces: scissors, cutters, spray bottles, needles, and punches. Then there are the scraps leftover from shape cutting but never thrown away.

Beth is, admittedly, not a neat freak. Her house reveals what our family lovingly refers to as "evidence of other priorities." Her workshop in particular can get messy fast. Staying over means pushing workbenches, boxes, and stools out of the way to lay an air mattress down. When I asked Beth about all the *stuff*, she said, "I think the mess is the point in a way. It's the single-minded focus of creativity. Who wants to stop that to clean or put things away?" (B. Sullivan, personal communication, April 28, 2016).

My cousin Chris, a welder and fabricator for a NASCAR team, crafts a range of furniture and lighting in his personal workshop. The first thing he said when I asked him for a photo was that it was too messy. My friend Eric, the theater technician, says the same. His workshop is loaded with building materials: wood, metals, acrylics, foams, graphics, and tools aplenty, like power tools, hand tools, computers, and more. He admits, "My shop has been messy at times, especially to certain people (such as my wife), but it's convenient and handy that way" (E. Dixon, personal communication, January 12, 2017). His wife happens to be one of my closest friends. On a recent phone call, she talked about how their family just moved to a smaller house, yet somehow Eric has more tools than ever.

I recently read the debut cookbook by Michelin-star chef Missy Robbins (2017) and was struck by how much a test kitchen is like a shop. Describing the mess of ingredients she stores in her tiny home kitchen, Robbins writes, "Knowing these ingredients are on hand doesn't curtail my creativity; instead, it allows me to make the spontaneous choices that I think are the most fun part of cooking" (p. 15). Necessity may be the mother of invention, but mess is the DNA.

Even for seasoned master, it's the mess that kindles new ideas. Beth comes across a scrap saved from the tiny sewing rooms of our grandmother and mother, and she integrates it into a new project. She used pieces of my mother's pink prom dress to make a *Grease* costume for her eldest daughter. What was left of that same prom dress then became a party dress for her younger daughter's school dance. Bob, the Navy captain I introduced in the previous chapter, remembers the day his lab students grabbed "a bowling ball to use as a pendulum" because it was just sitting there (R. Boyce, personal communication, January 6, 2017). Eric once came across a leftover piece of walnut, placed it in his lathe, and crafted a wand for one of his Harry-Potter-loving daughters.

Figure 4.1. Selecting scraps for a project

When we talk about mess in schools, we often focus on the art room. In her work, Lucy Calkins often likens the writing workshop to an art studio. And for good reason. Art teachers fill their spaces with a variety of materials that children can learn to choose from and interact with on their own. In fact, the art teachers at my sons' elementary school are shopping up their already loaded studios. They notified parents of a new self-directed program in their studios, in which they provide materials and opportunities to explore and play. To my delight, they call it *Workshop!* Their art workshop fosters creativity, independence, confidence, responsibility, and curiosity. Writing shop should foster creativity, independence, confidence, responsibility, and curiosity too. And it can, by making available the mess involved in writing.

The tools and materials in the writing shop seem, on the surface, self-explanatory. What does a writing workshop require? Writing utensils, primarily pencils and possibly pens. Paper in a few select forms: lined writer's notebooks, loose leaf, blank paper for drawings. Resources like dictionaries and word walls. A stapler for neatness. An easel could be handy. Even with limited items, any writing teacher can encourage her students' imaginations to spring to life and onto the page.

A more stocked writing workshop will offer greater variety, like oil pastels and permanent markers. Dot paints for illustrations. Some workshops have three-ring binders awaiting final versions and paper reinforcers to toughen up the holes. Maybe even correction fluid. My second-grade classroom closet held publication books of all kinds, including ones with hard white covers for illustrating.

Teacher Ann Marie Corgill (2008) describes her writing shop the way one might expect of an art studio. Her materials include crayons, markers, oil pastels, permanent markers for outlining (both black and colored), watercolors, highlighters, staplers/staples/staple removers, hole punches for two and three holes, paper reinforcers, transparent tape, glue sticks, scissors, book rings, paper clips, and a variety of paper choices (template paper, blank copy paper, and colored paper) (p. 40).

Now let's mess up the writing workshop even more. I don't advocate chaos or even clutter; in fact, unlike my sister, I'm a die-hard organizer, a neat-nick who keeps a tidy classroom and home. I inherited this from my mother, whose tiny sewing workshop, while overstuffed with supplies, was guided by the motto, *a place for everything and everything in its place.*

I advocate for a different kind of mess: a collection of seemingly random materials. Hodgepodge. What my mother called "potpourri." Each item is a tool, and students quickly learn the best tool for the job, the way they learn the best genre, shape, and tone for the audience and purpose of their piece.

To a writing shop, add some unexpected paper: parchment paper that crisps at the edges, graph paper that invites printing one letter per box, sticky notes that make it possible to move things around. Add other writing surfaces as well: dry erase boards, notecards, leaves, cardboard, vellum, and wood. Students can write notes on a shoebox, poetry on a shoestring.

Now add some unexpected utensils. One of my favorite writing craft mentors, Natalie Goldberg (1986), makes a big deal of writing utensils in *Writing Down the Bones*. She entreats writers to choose their utensils wisely, especially when it comes to speed: "It should be a fast-writing pen because your thoughts are always much faster than your hand" (p. 5). Gel pens are some of my favorites. I've asked students to trace all their adjectives in gel pen and see how they pop off the page the way they sing in our ears. If there's hardly any color to *see*, there's hardly any color in the writing. In one workshop, third graders discovered purple pencils and wrote with gusto for a few minutes. In another shop, students highlighted in neon colors the phrases they were especially proud of. Our writing students should try different writing utensils and test them out: What feels right in the hand? What makes an interesting mark on the page? Which utensil writes quiet words quietly? Which utensil shouts as loud as the words do? The writing utensil can spark imagination and change our thinking.

Add alternate uses for familiar items. I show students how they can choose a favorite mentor text, copy one line word for word, then replace each word one at a time, until several new sentences are formed. I encourage students to look at what's already close by and incorporate it: the pencil in hand might be a character; the chair might collapse; the teacher's shoes might suddenly begin to walk on their own. Open the dictionary not to look up the meaning of a word, but rather to land on a new word and use it to begin a new piece.

And what of those scraps, like the cutout shapes in my sister's quilting studio or the walnut lying around in Eric's theater shop? Writing benefits from randomness. New ideas emerge, new chances for collaboration pop up. Add to writing workshop photographs of large animals, world sites, and streets full of pedestrians. Add letter tiles and story starter cards. If you can't bring your students outdoors, bring the outdoors in: cups of dirt, bunches of grass, dried leaves, pebbles.

Inspired by Nicki Weiss's 1991 picture book *Surprise Box*, in which a young girl finds and stuffs an assortment of items (dandelions, dirt, even a worm) into a box as a gift for her grandmother, I often bring a surprise box of my own to writing workshop. I load it with miscellany from around my home: a snail-shaped doorstop, pink duct tape, loose board game pieces, a rubber duck. My students are welcome to dive in, for whatever purpose of writing and thinking. Sometimes I write mood words on index cards and separate them into "positive" and "negative" piles. Students consider how they feel that day and select positive or negative. Each takes a mood word from a face-down pile on the desk, then blindly pulls an object from the surprise box. They view, feel, and smell the objects as a means to wake up senses and trigger memories. They discuss, ask questions, and admit familiarity or foreignness. We talk about photo applications like Instagram, how choosing a particular filter evokes a certain mood, and how adjectives and verbs are the filters that evoke the moods they've pulled from the pile. Many joke about the unusual pairings: bungee cord and "ecstasy" or pink duct tape and "despair." Those who draft quickly write profound short pieces during workshop. Others think about the objects over the next few days until a story coalesces.

In a shop for students of education, I introduced Terry Tempest Williams's "An Unspoken Hunger" as a mentor text. The piece reads like a prose poem centering on the sensual and very human act of eating an avocado. We imagined Williams placing on her desk an avocado and an index card bearing the word "sensual." The teachers followed with new pieces of prose sparked by their seemingly mismatched objects and mood words. One of my students pulled "joyfulness" from the pile and a silicone spoon rest shaped like ravioli. She told me before writing that the ravioli made her feel hungry. She thought about hunger and what hunger and joy have in common. Then she wrote, within ten minutes, a memorable piece about the deep and binding love between ravioli and sauce. Pieces like this are wholly original and yet can be recalled again and again. When I'm in the kitchen cooking up a dinner, I think about the avocado and the ravioli, and I wonder which of the day's ingredients may be engaged in a secret affair.

My mother always gave me scraps of this and that when I became a teacher. "You'll find a use for it!" she said. And I always do. That day, I found a use for a silicone ravioli-shaped spoon rest. Better yet, *my student* found a use for it. It's the randomness of the objects, the mess in the box, that leads to surprising connections, thicker descriptions, and more vivid characters.

Add technology to the mess. I always have a handheld digital recorder in my shop. The cost was quite low and I use it for my personal writing projects as well. During one shop, when the early-spring air called the students outside rather than in, I showed my students how to use it. It's a simple device: press the red circle to record a new track, press the silver square to stop. I pressed record and began a story about a lion, then passed the recorder from student to student to add a line or two. Later, Valeria wanted to listen to the recording. She transcribed it word for word, then added details—the lion's name, his quest to find his roots, meeting a monkey. The recorded group story became the basis for her short but well-developed fiction.

If resources are available, add keyboards. Research shows keyboarding is valuable in the process of learning to write. Karin James, R. Joanne Jao, and Virginia Berninger (2016) studied the neuroscience on how the writing brain develops. They argue that handwriting instruction should be integrated with spelling and composing, which is one of the hallmarks of writing workshop (p. 124). They also note that while handwriting is the prime method for forming letters in early childhood and composing sentences in middle childhood, keyboarding grows advantageous as children grow older. The researchers conclude, "The goal of writing instruction in the Information Age should be developing hybrid writers who are adept with multiple writing tools including pens and keyboards" (p. 125).

I have countless stories of how mess has helped students in my writing shop, from four years old to twenty-four. Some of those stories I've already shared: second graders with their state floats, the storytelling trio with their white boards, Johnny with his lemon. In fact, I write this an hour after one of my three-year-old twins, whose name begins with R, wrote an R for the first time. He has been struggling to do so with pencils and crayons, even the extra-thick crayons the school's occupational therapist recommended. During free time I dumped an assortment of writing utensils on the table. In the mess, he found a green gel crayon, his favorite color, which is easy to grasp and glides more smoothly than a regular crayon. Before either of us knew it, he was drawing R after R after R, a huge smile on his face.

A fourth grader named Eliot always brought his own mess to shop, as so many children do. His backpack was loaded with small toys, stickers, rubber bands, and the detritus of a day at school. The latest toy trends can be a distraction, and schools often request that nothing of the kind be carried in. Backpack belongings can, however, be useful, even meaningful, additions to the mess of writing shop. Students can be taught to see their collection as stories waiting to be told. For Eliot, his fidget spinner, the "it" toy of the moment, became the central focus of his mystery about an orphan being the victim of a crime (see Figure 4.2).

Little Man

One scary, spooky, stormy, gloomy night a guy named Sharon was about to leave work. He hated when he had to work late. So when he left work he always felt like he was being stalked. One day he saw a little man walking by with a fidget spinner. One day the little man chased Sharon into the woods.

He wanted to quit his job but he needs money to pay college. He didn't get a scholarship and he had no parants to pay his college. Every night he thinks of his parents. They were killed at a doll store. No one knows what happened.

Today Sharon had to work late. When he was closing up the store and some one threw a fidget spinner and his missed. Then he saw a shadow chasing Sharon, threw more fidget spinners. Sharon fell down. The little man started hitting Sharon and put a sticky note on his back that said, "El Chucky was here."

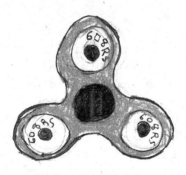

Figure 4.2. Little Man, by Eliot, grade 4

When drafting his story, Eliot used markers of different colors to proceed. The promise of a new color motivated him to continue down the page, adding a few sentences in one color, then adding a few more in another, until he sailed on to the next page.

Donald Graves (1983) urges us to see that the more mess we offer, the more learning we do as teachers. We gain valuable knowledge about our students by providing a mess and watching how they use it. In other words, as masters, we know to sit back and observe how students play. In a first-grade shop, for example,

> Many kinds of writing implements are available: crayons, pencils—large and small, short and long, wide and thin. Put the materials in a small can or caddy where the children can choose the implements with which they are most familiar. It is useful information for the teacher to see which implements are chosen and just how the children use the page. Some will put their names on it, some just letters, or a few words and sentences. Some may only draw. Others will start in the lower right hand corner and move in column form up the page; a few may even scribble. All believe they are writing. (p. 18)

The presence of mess also invites students to interact in the way identical pencils do not. When a student finds the one gel pen that includes glitter, another student inevitably wants to use it too. What follows is the best kind of off-the-page learning: What is the most appropriate and effective way to ask a peer to borrow something? How can we organize turns? Could we compliment each other on how we used the material? When writing time is done for the day, students must replace the items. It's more than just popping pencils into cups. Mess demands teamwork and organization.

Mess is the best way to invite all writers to the table as well. The ubiquitous pencil and paper can spark terror in those students who consider themselves non-writers. I refer to this terror as "blank-page syndrome." But what about a dry erase board and red marker? What about a felt-tip pen or a giant marker? Have a student with "BPS" copy a favorite line in glitter pen. No more blank page. I tell my students this all the time: if reluctance builds because of fear of the blank page, ask a friend to say a random word and copy that word onto your page. Write it again. Write it vertical. Write it backwards. Write a rhyming word. Notice reluctance fading as the page fills up.

Additionally, Colleen Cruz (2008) suggests multiple materials for students who seem reluctant or claim their hands hurt (my eldest son's chief complaint when practicing letters). Ensuring the mess includes a variety of writing utensils, surfaces, and supports, like soft mats under paper or inclined clipboards, can catch those students who otherwise struggle with grip, posture, and pressure.

One of my eldest son's first preschool teachers collected random materials for her students. When I asked her about how she views teaching writing, she scoffed at prescribed stories and talked about having her students slice up graphic organizers to move words around. Often, something born of gently guided exploration came home in my son's backpack. I remember a piece of blue construction paper, cut roughly into an oval, with 20 or so wiggle eyes glued to the center. He said it's a fish, and he wanted it to have "lots and lots of eyes for seeing." Out spilled his whole fish tale, loosely based on the mentor text *This Is Not My Hat* by Jon Klassen (2012). His story was initiated not by a story starter or even with words. His story began with those eyes. Once my son saw all those wiggle eyes in a heap, he *had* to use them. And once he glued so many of them down, he *had* to invent a reason for his fish to need them. My son was just learning how to glue and had practiced with scissors for a few weeks. His extra-visual fish, sprung from his imagination and the tools and materials available for writing, also showed use of symbols and fine-motor skills, plus a sense of humor.

When I first started collecting my writing into a professional portfolio, I met with an established mentor writer about my work. She told me my writing was too tight. It was well written and organized, but too tight. "You need to learn to roll around in the language," she told me. "Mess things up." We want our writing students to roll around in language, an act of both enthusiasm and courage. To begin her short story "Draft," Deb Olin Unferth (2016) writes, "Everywhere she looks she finds pieces of the story she wanted to write." Frank McCourt (1998) echoes this idea of rolling in the mess when describing his writing process that led to *Angela's Ashes*: "It was kind of a mosaic: bits would come to me and I'd put them down" (p. 78). We want our students to create, in the end, organized stories—but first, we need to let them roll around in the mess.

Let's learn from the art teachers, who tell us that much of the time, their students just want the chance to cut, glue, punch holes, tape, string, sew, staple, stack, draw, and paint. Our school's art teachers say that children beg for this open time. Whenever my sons come home messy with paint, glue, and stickers, I tell them a messy shirt is a sign of a good day. After all, they got to muck about all morning—how lucky!

SPLINTERS AND STEAM

Sense Stimulation

> What people don't realize is that writing is physical. It doesn't have to do with thought alone. It has to do with sight, smell, taste, feeling, with everything being alive and activated. (Goldberg, 1986, p. 50)

The term "multisensory" is one of the most common words in education research and advocacy today. Since physician Samuel Orton and educator Anna Gillingham premiered multisensory reading instruction in the early 20th century, numerous programs have grown to help teachers guide their young students through multisensory reading instruction. I took a summer workshop on Phyllis Bertin and Eileen Perlman's (1998) Preventing Academic Failure curriculum, for example, which is a multisensory approach to literacy learning. The guidebook begins: "Learning to read is the most difficult cognitive task faced by children" and explains the many functions involved (p. 1). Instruction is most successful when all these functions are integrated. As in a writing workshop, aspects of reading are not separated; rather, reading, phonics, handwriting, spelling, and grammar are folded into the same program.

While it is important to recognize how reading and writing shops are similar in their multisensory approaches, in this chapter, I discuss not the conventional understanding of the term "multisensory" but rather the fact that multiple senses are tapped in all shops. Thus, I use the term "sense stimulation" to distinguish from the widely known multisensory programs. When I refer to sense stimulation, I mean the activation of all our senses in the context of shop. Sense stimulation may be the single most obvious element of all workshops, yet it is something we take for granted unless we explicitly focus on it.

When I transitioned out of elementary school teaching and into writing and the teaching of writing, my first significant work—so significant I am publishing a book on the topic—was the story of how I lost my childhood memory and, as an adult, tried to find it again. I wanted to capture my

© KONINKLIJKE BRILL NV, LEIDEN, 2019 | DOI:10.1163/9789004397880_005

childhood in writing, the way so many of my favorite memoirists do, but I didn't have any memory to rely on. Armed with family stories, photographs, and items stored in my mother's house since childhood, I tried to recreate what I couldn't remember. A particular memory I wanted to regain was of a family visit to the Jersey shore where my father grew up. My sisters tell me we rented a cottage near the beach, close to our grandmother, aunts, uncles, and cousins. We spent hours sculpting sand castles and wading into the water, clutching our father's hands, while our mother, always in a hand-made dress and never in the ocean, laid out plentiful picnic supplies.

I have photos from the trip. Most show a line of little girls standing in the surf, wearing matching bikinis with bright red ties. This is particularly surprising to me, since I have developed an adverse reaction to saltwater and can't even wade now without breaking out in an itchy red rash. My father is in some of the photos. In my writing, I wanted to animate him and animate us together as a family. So while working on my memory story, I'd keep a small container of Coppertone suntan lotion, the sunscreen we used back then, in my bag, and take it out when I wanted to meditate on the beach, search for the memory, imagine the scene, write it down. I drafted in mechanical pencil, since memory, especially mine, was impermanent. I wrote the first parts in a small notebook with a soft quilted cover my sister made for me. Using my senses and imagination, I created something on paper that, after a long while, satisfied me as a stand-in for a memory. The piece never would have come to be without the photos, the pencil, and the sweet coconut smell of Coppertone.

There may be nothing more telling of shop than sense stimulation. We know we have entered an alternate space by the dramatic shift in sight, sound, and smell. Chef Missy Robbins (2017) talks of entering the kitchen space for the first time: "I loved everything about it: the energy, the smells, the food, the artistry, the order mixed in with the chaos. ... This was different. The people were different. The expectations were different. It was exhilarating" (p. 9). My friend Jenni, a craftsperson very much like my mother and sister, describes her workshop:

> There's a rhythm to any sort of making, whether it's the clickity-clack of laptop keys, the whirring and pulsing of a sewing machine, or the whisper of yarn pulled from a skein and wound around a needle again and again and again until a shape begins to emerge. It almost always smells like coffee or tea; those are my most productive beverages. Occasionally it smells like wine, but only if it's an easy project. (J. Eaton, personal communication, January 23, 2017)

Jenni is also an English teacher and a writer. The way she describes her workshop—I can't imagine a more inviting space in which to make things.

Similarly, Michael Crawford (2009), while narrating how he left corporate work for shop work, notes that the senses were the first sign of such a significant change. "I would come home from work and my wife would sniff at me," writes Crawford. "She'd say 'carbs' or 'brakes' as she learned to identify the various solvents used in cleaning different parts of a motorcycle. Leaving a sensible trace, my workday was at least imaginable to her" (pp. 24–25).

Isn't that the whole point of writing? To write something that is imaginable to the reader? No matter what the content or purpose, readers should imagine something when they read: a scene, a place, a character, the way something feels, the way something works, the sound of a voice, the solution to a problem, a path to agreement with the writer, a clear reason to disagree with the writer, a new idea. Good writing ensures that readers imagine all these things.

This is why writing teachers borrow sensory words to describe good writing. We ask our students to *show* rather than tell and detail their work using all five *senses*. We expect sentence *fluency*, how the language *sounds* to our ears, whether it has *rhythm* and *flow*. We want *spoken dialogue*. We ask students to keep *audience* in mind and allow their unique *voices* to spring from the page. We help them develop a main idea and add details like *branches* of a tree. We help them organize, so their main idea comes full *circle*. Authors Brenda Miller and Suzanne Paola (2005) remind us that just as our brains convert sensory input into data, we writers must convert that data into words for our readers. Miller and Paola write, "We experience the world through our senses. We must translate that experience into the language of the senses as well" (p. 7). Author Sue William Silverman (2009) refers to writing as "following a sensory trail" until we find the right "savory words" (p. 10, 17).

Feel, sound, shape, smell, taste … we want our students' writing, in all genres and for all purposes, to be anything but static. We must, therefore, provide a sense-full workshop environment that triggers dynamic writing. In a writing shop, senses are tools. Senses are talked about as tools and treated as tools. And as such, senses are stimulated so that the tools are turned on. How can a writer write of a smell without using her smell tool? How can a writer describe the feeling of a fabric without feeling fabric?

Writer Louise DeSalvo (2014) comments in her book *The Art of Slow Writing* just how bland her writing becomes when she is sitting at a familiar desk. During a trip to Mexico, when writing about her father's stay on an island during World War II, she realized through the sensory experience of being at a hotel overlooking the ocean that she needed to understand just how it felt to be on the island. And to understand that feeling, she needed to experience it through the senses: the heat, the feeling of the sand, whether drinkable water was on hand.

> As I tried describing what I saw, I realized that when I write indoors, I rarely pause and look up from my work and see what's around me—my study is too familiar for me to take notice of it. But when I write elsewhere, I notice where I am, and that act of witnessing my surroundings slows me down and enriches the act of writing without taking me away from my work. (p. 65)

Experiencing the world through the senses is the most natural human act. Writing shops should not divorce young writers from this act, especially when good writing intends to provoke the same act in its readers: to experience a piece of writing with all the senses. To create a sense-full shop, I incorporate a variety of sense stimulations, including the following.

Objects: I describe grab bags of miscellaneous objects in Chapter 4 on mess. These objects are magnificent sensory stimulators. I have students pull objects at random and study them for color, texture, weight, smell, and sometimes even taste. Students generate sensory word lists, which in turn spark descriptions. Sometimes students use objects to create new writing, while other times they relate objects to a piece they are writing. Students might insert a random object into a half-written story and figure out how the characters will respond. I've asked students to find an object in the writing shop or observe one out the window and write a single-sentence description about it. That description is then used as the basis of a new piece or is transferred to another piece the student is working on. Sometimes that description is transferred to a different object or even to a person. Once, an education student in my shop described a simple rock, then realized how apt the description was for one of her college professors, someone she both feared and trusted. She changed out the subject of the sentence, and her teacher became, if I remember correctly, "hard with a hint of bright crystals." As I discuss earlier, treasures often appear in backpacks and, rather than becoming distractions, can be used to stimulate the senses. A typical student backpack itself is a sensory medley.

Reenactment: Students love to act out stories. Acting out their own writing for each other helps them hear the loud parts and see the scared, confused, proud, or excited looks on faces. To really shop up reenactment, I have students use different tools and materials to enhance their oral performance;

for example, I ask students to provide a drumroll with pencils on the table when an exciting part is coming up, or ring a bell each time a sentence ends with an exclamation point. Listeners tune in and learn how word choices and sentence structures create the drumroll effect in print, and why certain parts of a story should be emphasized with the written version of a bell's ring. Often, when a student presents an idea but is stuck on how to begin, I have the student reenact with as much sense stimulation as possible. Like Joaquim, kicking his own shin in order to describe how it feels, reenactment can help writers get unstuck.

Scenter: I love to bring in a tray full of re-purposed spice jars, something I have long called a "scenter." Each holds a natural, strong-smelling substance (school-approved to avoid allergy triggers) that can help students recall memories, spark imaginations, or foster discussion about what they love and hate about certain scents. Some of the scents I include are banana, orange, popcorn, yogurt of various flavors, burned wood, sawdust, lavender, jasmine, vanilla, lemon, cinnamon, musk, mint, and rose. The scenter invites conversation about which smells are strong, which are pleasant, which are offensive, and which connect to place. I was delighted when one student exclaimed how vanilla reminded him of his father, as I've held onto my own father's pipe for its remaining tobacco smell. I remember when two students argued over whether "spicy" is a smell word or taste word. The student who thought it was a taste word decided to try it out as smell: "I can smell the spicy pepperoni."

Figure 5.1. Sniffing soaked cotton balls from the scenter

Snacks: I often give my shop students a school-approved snack, such as pretzels or graham crackers, and ask them to savor the treats and hunt for new words to describe them. I ask questions about what happens to the snacks when they sit in the mouth for too long or are crushed between two fingers before eating. Crunching on a snack can help writers fall into a spell just as easily as it can help distract writers who need a break. Sometimes the food becomes the focus. Angeles, one of my fifth graders, loved Goldfish crackers, wrote a story about them, and taped several of the snacks into her notebook. It's one piece I wish I'd been able to copy and save, but the crumbs finally got the better of the page.

Music and sound: Sometimes, a little music stirs students to think in new ways. Sometimes, music provides a comforting barrier between writer and environment. I also like to have students investigate shop objects for the sounds they make. I often let older students play various sounds available on my cell phone for call and message alerts and translate them into words. Students can also fill in their own sounds and ideas by flipping through wordless picture books (such as *Wave* [2008] by Suzy Lee) or watching short films without dialogue (such as Pixar's *For the Birds* [2000]). With the latter, students discuss how the music tells the story, and use that understanding to add musical traits like rhyme, pattern, beat, and tempo to their writing. I have students close their eyes and tune in to the sounds around them, listen through the window to the sounds of the street, listen to each other whisper, speak in a high pitch, speak slowly or speak quite loudly. I play clips of ambient sounds, like water rushing or dense traffic or cats purring.

I once read that writer Barb Johnson (2011) uses the playback feature on computers. "When I've been working on something for a while, for long enough that I can't really tell what it says anymore," she tells fellow writer Cynthia Newberry Martin, "I like to save it as a .pdf and then hit 'read aloud.' Listening to a robot voice read the material makes me focus on the words, what's actually on the page." I plan to make this my next sensory move in the shop.

In isolation, these suggestions may seem unexceptional. But in combination, they point to one potent way we can shop up our writing workshops, as well as the reasons why we must do so. Sense stimulation is inherently playful and inclusive. The proof is in the pudding, so to speak. Kleydi, a writer in a third-grade writing shop, transformed from somewhat reluctant writer to self-acclaimed author once she focused on her senses in shop. She created a sense-filled piece, which had her walking out of shop telling me, "I want to write books!" (see Figure 5.2).

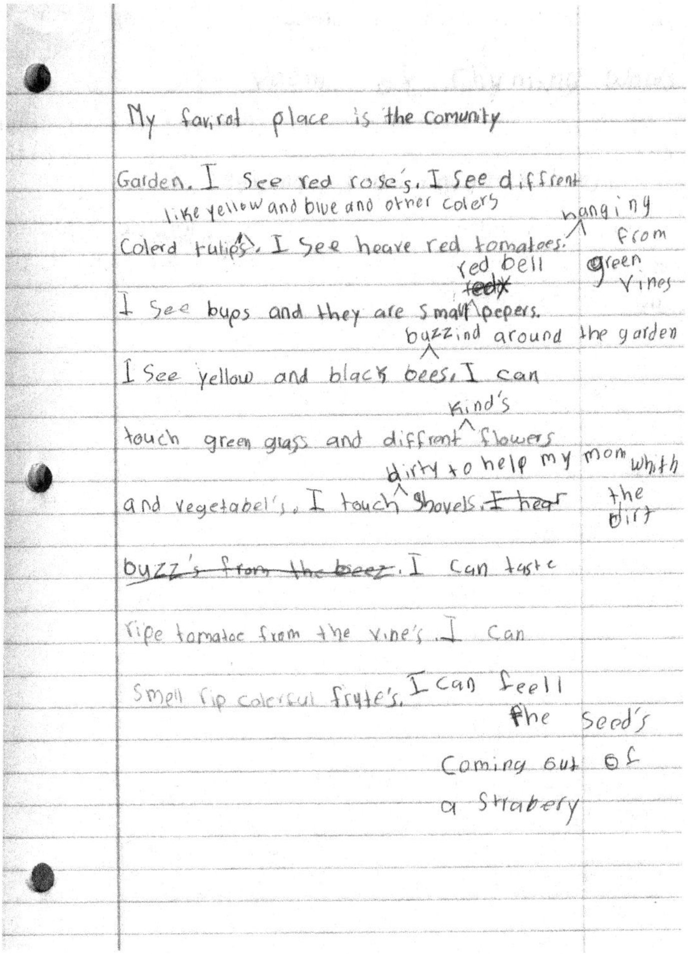

My favrot place is the comunity
Garden. I see red rose's. I see diffrent
like yellow and blue and other colers
Colerd tulips. I see heave red tomatoes. hanging from
red bell green
~~teolx~~ vines
I see bups and they are small pepers.
buzzind around the garden
I see yellow and black bees, I can
kind's
touch green grass and diffront flowers
dirty to help my mom whith
and vegetabel's. I touch shovels. I hear the dirt
buzz's from the beez. I can taste
ripe tomatoe from the vine's. I can
smell rip colerful fryte's. I can feell
the seed's
coming out of
a strabery

Figure 5.2. Garden piece, by Kleydi, grade 3

I love the scene in the movie *Ratatouille* (2007) when Remy the rat, a surprisingly talented chef, closes his eyes and imagines brightly lit swirling shapes as he munches on strawberries and cheese. "Each flavor was totally unique," Remy says. "But combine one flavor with another, and something new was created." My students do the same with sounds and smells and tastes, imagining them as brightly lit swirling shapes, which they translate into words to create something new.

Imagine a writing workshop humming with soft sounds of students choosing utensils and paper, students measuring items or feeling them with closed eyes to get the details right. Imagine students exchanging writing prompts with each other. Swapping a gel pen for a colored pencil, choosing between recording themselves in audio and typing on a tablet, donning costume pieces and acting out certain parts to get the mood and dialogue down, opening jars of scents to trigger memories and ideas, putting on headphones to listen to a bit of music or a section of an audio book for inspiration. Imagine students just wondering at the window. This is the writing shop, richly and creatively sensory, that will draw out of students what makes them unique observers, thinkers, and personalities.

CHAPTER 6

RAISE THE BENCH

Workspace Variety

Any space where you put pen to paper, hand to keyboard, voice to recorder—or simply sit and dream your way into words—can be a writing space. (McClanahan, 2001, p. 24)

At six years old, my eldest son is obsessed with trains. Aside from playing at the train table we inherited from my sister, he sleeps in train bedding, dressed as a train engineer one Halloween, and loves nothing more than to visit our local train station. Often, he asks to watch track-building videos on YouTube, where other train-loving families show viewers how they build complex tracks that rise and loop. My son observes, wide-eyed, runs to the table to connect two ends or make a turn, returns to our iPad to watch more video, then moves to the floor to try building something bigger and more elaborate. His ideas often are sparked by something external (the video) and he must try it right away, apply it, change it, make it his own. In any given ten-minute span, he may work at three different surfaces.

I do the same thing when I'm writing. I move around. I take frequent breaks to fold laundry, stretch, or look at a new object and describe it to get my mind going. I especially like to prop my feet up. So I don't get a lot of writing done at my desk. Reading, research, revision, sure. But writing is done in different spaces and in different positions.

When I first started writing professionally, a mentor read some of my work and asked me to clarify a few ideas she didn't quite understand. After we conferred, she said I spoke about those ideas far more clearly than I wrote about them, and a good start to revision would be to simply speak into a recorder and then transcribe my own words onto the page. I've remembered that tip and continue to use it today. In fact, I wrote parts of this book while sitting in my car and speaking into my phone's voice memo application. An idea would hit at the most unlikely moment, and I wanted to remember it later. I'd spend a minute or two paused at a stop sign, my foot glued to the brake pedal, speaking my thoughts until someone pulled up behind me.

© KONINKLIJKE BRILL NV, LEIDEN, 2019 | DOI:10.1163/9789004397880_006

My brain was connecting ideas much faster in speech than my fingers could have put them to paper.

My good friend Cheryl, a poet and architecture writer, used to work closely with Ligon Flynn, a well-known architect based in North Carolina. Cheryl's work as a writer for Flynn was contingent on her exposure to and immersion in his content. To her, the architecture shop was more than a place of business; it was the only space in which she could actually write what she needed to for her job. "I loved being around all the models, drawings, blueprints, scratch paper—the stuff of drawing buildings," she told me. "My workspace, with two tables, a bookshelf, books over every square inch of space, an OED ready—this was my workshop. The architect's workspace inspired my workspace" (C. Wilder, personal communication, April 30, 2016).

Similarly, my friend Eric's scenery workshop contains workspaces suited to his needs, including a space designated for acrylics and high workbenches to save his back from having to bend too much. (At six-foot-nine, Eric needs those tall benches.)

In my shops, students know they can—and often should—move. Sometimes I invite a student to move when I can tell movement is necessary. One afternoon, a thunderstorm struck so fast, all the students jumped. Edgar and Alondra wanted to watch. Of course they did—so did I. So I led all willing students to the hallway where the windows were larger. We watched for a few minutes. Then, back at her desk, Alondra changed direction in her writing. She began a new piece about thunderstorms by likening thunder to the growl of a hungry belly ("stumitk grolling"). I did not need to teach a lesson on similes or descriptive language. I needed to show her the storm through the window, so she could show the storm through her words (see Figure 6.1).

Angeles, a fourth grader who was born in Mexico but moved to the United States with her family when she was still a baby, wanted to write from a place of anger and fear, but couldn't get anything down on paper. Not a word. She was grappling with the news and stories she was hearing from her parents and others in her community about rising deportations and growing anti-immigration sentiment. I gave her the digital recorder and showed her how to work the buttons. She recorded a poem in two parts, one about love and the other about hate, two halves of a whole picture: her love of Mexico and her hatred of the politics surrounding immigration. Then, to transcribe, Angeles crawled under a table. The whole writing experience unfolded for Angeles under there, which became her workspace for the rest of shop.

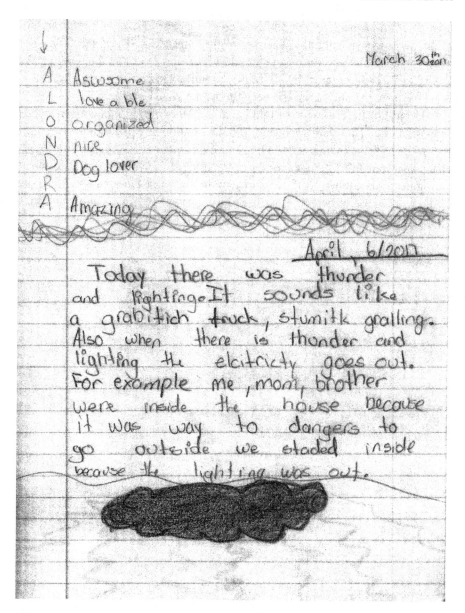

Figure 6.1. Thunderstorm writing, by Alondra, grade 3

Angeles chose the digital recorder because it was the best tool to get her charged words onto the page. She was both working and playing. She loved pressing the buttons on the recorder, watching the red light glow, hearing her own voice speak back to her. She giggled while she did it, even as the content of her writing was something far from giggling about. Then she found the best workspace to suit her needs. She drew comfort from the table above her as she wrote of her fear of losing family members to deportation. It was as if the table protected her from the very threat she was describing.

Contrary to Angeles, who sought isolation, other children become nervous to work alone. These children should have options to work in pairs or small groups, or to settle themselves next to a good friend to work side by side. Each group, without fail, includes at least one student who can only write when sitting near the teacher, as if proximity to the shop master is an essential part of the workspace. When creating the writing shop, we must establish spaces where young writers can think, play, build, and write alone and together.

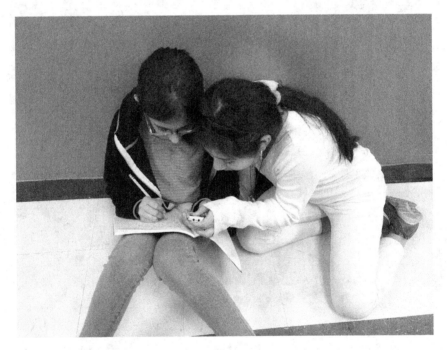

Figure 6.2. Students write in the hallway with the digital recorder

Elementary-school teacher Ann Marie Corgill (2008) discusses what young students deserve to have in their writing workshops. She prioritizes workspace variety, from conversation-friendly seating arrangements to gathering spaces for sharing time. One characteristic she lists caught my eye when I first read it: "An environment that values community and the exchange of ideas rather than isolation and self-promotion" (p. 27). Many industries see the value in just such a workspace. On an episode of his design and architecture podcast *99% Invisible*, host Roman Mars (2016) talks about how urban designers seek both variety and comfort in their city plans. City officials hope pedestrians, walking through the well-designed city, will randomly meet up, making for more rewarding and productive interactions.

In his work on writing conferences, Carl Anderson (2000) devotes two pages to discussing where exactly to meet with students about their writing. To Anderson, the setting is as important as the content of the conference, as it "influences students' willingness to talk with us, as well as the tone of our conversations with them" (p. 156). Through his guidebook, Anderson taught me to always meet students where they are, "at their desks or tables, even on the floor in the corner if that's where they're writing" (p. 156). The first time I read that passage, I realized that if I'm to conference with students wherever they are writing, I need to back up a step and create all the differences spaces in which they can write. They must feel comfortable writing in different spaces and moving between them, so they can be comfortable speaking with me about their writing in those spaces. Anderson goes on to clarify we should meet students at eye level, meaning, we should sit or kneel, get down in the same workspace with students rather than loom over them (p. 157). As with the other elements of shop, a variety of workspaces, the ways we allow our students to utilize those spaces, and the ways we visit our students in those spaces, are critical.

One semester, a YouTube video called "The People vs. The School System" made the rounds among my students. Musician, speaker, and social media personality Richard Williams (2016), using his stage name Prince Ea, created the video to lampoon the current U.S. education system for its outdated methods. Early in the video, which is set in a courtroom, he shows a "judge" and "jury" a photo of a modern smart phone, followed by a phone from 150 years ago. "Big difference, right?" Williams asks. Then he repeats the bit with a car from today and a car from decades past. Finally, he comes upon a classroom from today: students sitting in chairs at their desks, all facing the teacher at the front of the room. Next picture? A classroom from 150 years ago that looks remarkably the same. The jury gasps. "Now ain't that a shame?"

My students debated. Is it alarming that classrooms still look and feel like they always have? Perhaps not. The human body still needs chairs. My students and I laughed when discussing this undeniable reality: our bodies have not evolved much in the past century. We bend and sit exactly as we have for hundreds of thousands of years. And no matter how modern a classroom or workspace becomes, gravity remains. We need flat surfaces to hold items so they don't roll or slide to the floor.

Plus, so many classrooms *have* changed. Even classrooms with all those desks and chairs now include technology and features that could not have been possible 150 years ago. Interactive boards, laptops for students, and open meeting space are growing more common. Flexible seating can be found in some classrooms.

At the same time, the video touches on a broader point: in every classroom, has the workspace changed *enough*? Does the workspace adequately function based on the needs of the class? A writing shop holds chairs and desks. But that's not enough. Not for writing in this century. Not for the writing done by our variety of students. Not for writing inspirational work.

The time of neatly rowed desks is not necessarily over. Neatly rowed desks have their function. But workspaces must evolve to serve multiple new functions. We all must move. If a student doesn't feel free to stand at the window and consider a storm in order to capture the right sound for her story, to study the movement of a squirrel and wonder why one squirrel is gray and another is black, to watch how different drivers handle a growing pothole, to imagine where the steam from the neighboring building's roof vents is coming from, to listen to a solitary unidentified sound and assign it to magical creature, that student's writing will be as predictable as the neat row in which she sits, as stiff as the chair back that holds her.

GET YOUR GOGGLES

Safety Procedures

A teacher must be certain that young writers feel safe before asking them to shape imagination into stories or to place memories and deep feelings into poem lines. (Tannenbaum & Bush, 2005, p. 1)

My husband and I took our three boys to visit friends one New Year's Day. They'd just bought a new house that provided a little more room for their two growing daughters. As we toured, I noticed a number of hand-made furniture pieces: corner desks, tables, bookshelves loaded with literature. Loft beds from the old house had even been reassembled in the new basement; the girls sleep there when guests stay in their bedrooms upstairs.

My twin sons, who were two at the time, love to explore new places. In the basement playroom, the boys found every cabinet, drawer, and door to open and close, again and again. The simple game: one would say "bye-bye" to the other, close the door, then open it again and dissolve into giggles at seeing his brother waiting for him on the other side. As it happened, their favorite door for this game led to the woodshop. My trained parenting eyes darted around, looking for hazards. Circular saw? Mounted to the center of a workbench and out of the reach of little fingers. Sharp-edged tools? Hanging high on walls or secured in boxes. No loose wires, no slippery spills, no heavy cans waiting to be tipped. Of course, I wasn't surprised. Our friends are both teachers, and with young children, they're careful. I felt relieved that my little ones could play freely in the woodshop. And I was delighted to stand in the space where all the lovely furniture pieces had been crafted.

In any workshop, safety is paramount. Safety equipment, such as goggles and masks, are hung on hooks, ready for student use the moment they walk in. Sharp and heavy tools live in designated spots, and students are taught how to be safe *around* them before they are taught how to use them. Ventilation is considered. Machines are maintained so broken parts do not jeopardize the work. Ear protection is available when those machines get loud. And with all those machines that require power, electrical wiring is carefully planned so

© KONINKLIJKE BRILL NV, LEIDEN, 2019 | DOI:10.1163/9789004397880_007

no single socket becomes overwhelmed. Critically, students are taught how to use the equipment and when to steer clear. Shop teachers ensure that their students can become independent.

Figure 7.1. Charlotte, grade 4, irons carefully

When he first started working at a scenery shop at the University of Illinois, woodworker Nick Offerman (2016) recognized safety for the first time. "It was my first run-in with shop safety as well," he writes, "learning the proper equipment and techniques to use around the massive milling machines and the treacherous table saw" (p. 5). The word "treacherous" here should be emphasized. Because just as a scenery shop can be treacherous to fingers and arms, a writing shop without safety is treacherous to confidence, learning, and emotional health.

Figure 7.2. Mitchell, grade 4, works with a sewing machine

To understand why safety is critical in writing shop, we can turn to professional writers. One of the greatest writers of our time, Toni Morrison (1998), has this to say about feeling scared:

> When you first start writing—and I think it's true for a lot of beginning writers—you're scared to death that if you don't get that sentence right that minute it's never going to show up again. And it isn't. But it doesn't matter—another one will, and it'll probably be better. And I don't mind writing badly for a couple of days because I know I can fix it—and fix it again and again and again, and it will be better. (p. 200)

We must tune in to such writers—the famous ones—who share their stories of fear. And we must write too; we must sit in own fear and write. Because without understanding what our students go through when they are asked to share their intimate thoughts, we risk forgetting just how vulnerable we are asking our students to be. And without establishing safety procedures in our writing shops, we risk squandering the opportunity for students to learn how to fix the things they've made.

One year I had a student who resisted writing. In truth, he resisted just about every aspect of school: the curriculum, the routine, socializing with many of his peers. But in writing, his resistance was stalwart. Cemented. Finally, after a class discussion about how we can lay our problems down on paper as a means to discover possible solutions, he wrote,

My problem.

> My problem is what I have to write for this assignment. I do not want to write this because it is my own business and my own problem. How would you feel if you had to share your difficulties with everybody? I know everybody has difficulties, but I don't want to talk about mine. .So I don't want to write about this subject. Privacy is important to me. And I would rather write about root beer.

Figure 7.3. My problem, by a student in grade 4

I was thrilled he wrote something. Plus, he had a point. How *would* I feel if I had to share my difficulties with everybody? We must understand what vulnerability feels like before we can establish the safety procedures our students need.

While instructing teachers in writing workshop, I ask what qualities make for the most ready and willing writing students. The top quality is always "feels safe." I ask what qualities make for the most effective writing spaces. Again, the group consensus is "safety." Students who feel comfortable, safe, and supported will contribute to the community in positive ways that, in turn, ensure other students feel comfortable, safe, and supported.

To emphasize the need for safety, I have teachers write personal stories in journals. Then, we run through a series of exercises: sharing those stories with one other person, sharing them with the table, sharing them with the whole group, vocalizing our desire not to share, requesting not to share by quietly folding the page over, and more. We discuss what all of these exercises feel like, and we tease out the raw fear that often accompanies writing. We delineate specific things we're afraid of: blank-page syndrome, looking foolish, making mistakes, sharing something personal and being teased for it. Once we name the fears, we can honor them, understand why they arise, and work against indulging them with thoughts that prevent us from writing.

What does safety look like in writing shop? We teach students how to use the actual tools of writing, from staplers to three-hole punches. With younger students, this kind of direct safety training is as important as it is in a woodshop. More, we teach students how to honor each contribution.

Any writing instruction worth its salt teaches students of all ages how to respond appropriately to peer writing: listen carefully, explain how you receive the writing, ask questions, and make thoughtful suggestions. Students are taught specific writer language to use when discussing each other's writing work. Trust is essential. Privacy must be honored. The more students write, and in shop they write all the time, the more they learn about each other and develop trust.

Students should know they can draw, color, graffiti their notebooks, build with materials, search for new shop items to describe, read someone else's work, read a mentor text, look for inspiration out the window, and think. I tell my students when they feel stuck in writing to copy a sentence or two, sometimes a whole paragraph, from a mentor text. Word for word. It helps students get into the writing groove, avoid BPS, and see why they like the mentor work so much. Writing doesn't always look like writing.

One of my third-grade shop students, Joaquim, was typically an enthusiastic writer. His hand stayed up throughout mini-lessons and his mind seemed to generate limitless ideas. But Joaquim was having a bad day. He was quiet, sullen even. Something had happened on the way into shop between Joaquim and Allison, and Joaquim was upset. Something had happened earlier in the day as well, though I was unable to coax it out of him. But Joaquim did reveal he had recently visited the LEGOLAND® Discovery Center in Westchester, New York, with his family. After many labored minutes, he produced a page with the heading JOAQUIM LAND on the top. Then he added a small sketch on the bottom right, which seemed to indicate a pizza shop. And he was done. That was fine with me. He had contributed what he could for the day—a drawing that represented a recent experience—and no additional "writing" would have helped him learn something new (see Figure 7.4).

Recall Angeles, whose fear for her family's safety outside the school was affecting her ability to engage in shop. When she felt safe under that table, she was able to dictate and then squeeze out a poem that outlined her fears and emotions.

When I participate in a workshop as a writer, I become frustrated when sharing time means only one thing: share your work. So I teach my shop students that sharing *may* mean sharing a new piece, or at least one favorite line. But it may mean sharing a new skill, a reaction to the process, a frustration, a triumph, or a question. Sharing may mean predicting what one will write the next day or talking about a mentor text that inspired a new piece. Sharing may mean paying a compliment to another writer. List all the ways students may share, ask them to contribute more ways, and keep

Figure 7.4. Joaquim Land, by Joaquim, grade 3

the list handy to remind students that all the ways they participate in sharing time are valuable to the shop.

Throughout the literature on writing workshop is evidence of shop teachers prioritizing safety. Teacher Brett Stonebrink (2001) writes about how his writing workshop finally drew out a piece of writing from a student named James who had been resisting for over a year. Giving James complete autonomy of choice, even, as as second grader, to write about a slasher movie, made him feel safe that his ideas and interests had a place in the shop. "At the moment James opened up to me," writes Stonebrink," I sensed that he was expecting to be rejected as he had been so many times before. My acceptance of and interest in his writing topic may have surprised him" (p. 26). To make this moment possible, Stonebrink had worked hard. "The harmony of the writer's workshop doesn't come without a price," he writes (p. 26). Students must learn early on how shop works and how to independently follow and protect the routine: "Managing the writer's workshop is maddening if you're alone. Every person in the room, regardless of height, should share the responsibility" (p. 26). Once that foundation is established, students feel safe.

Mr. Bangs, featured in Donald Graves's (1983) work, discusses safety procedures as well. When he first implemented writing workshop, he laid out a very specific pattern of response to writing, "an appropriate pattern that protected against hurt: receive the piece; ask the author if the reception was accurate, and then go on to questions" (p. 38).

In Nancy Shelton's (2007) workshop, including students with special needs meant focusing on community building. The community in writing workshop is built on both sameness (all are writing here) and difference (all have different abilities, styles, habits, points of view, and experiences). Her safety procedures were put in place early and firmly. This particularly benefited the special-needs students, who "often thought they were the only ones who struggled with learning" (p. 334).

Writing workshop teachers should make direct connections between the safety procedures in their shops and those in other shops. Doing so reminds the teachers why safety is as much as part of the writing shop as it is a woodshop. And it helps students see safety in concrete ways. They are much more likely to achieve safety if the somewhat murky idea of "we are careful with words" is likened to "we are careful with tools." Tell your students that just as we protect our eyes and hands, we protect our ideas and feelings. And I am not above letting students wear actual safety goggles when they read each other's writing. I can't think of a more direct way to teach students how to handle writing with care.

ALL HANDS ON DECK

Technical Skills

No matter what the purpose, writing is a craft. This means that it can be learned and its skills developed to a high degree through informed practice. (Cunningham, 2009, p. 11)

I worked with a student named Arthur for his sixth and seventh grade years, as he struggled as a writer. He was full—possibly overfull—of ideas and could talk at length and in hyperbole, but could not yet translate those ideas into clear prose. So I applied shop elements to our writing sessions. One afternoon, Arthur was bubbling with a story from gym class. A classmate had challenged a teacher to a soccer shootout. To Arthur and his friends, it was an epic battle between coach and player that unfolded, with shocking twists and a dramatic finish. Sensing that if I asked him to sit and write the story in that moment I might unwittingly plug up the dam, I decided to type it for him while he paced the room, narrating with wildly expressive hands. Then, without changing a word, we printed the story. I challenged him to cut it down to a finite number of words: get it below 500 words, then below 400, then, finally, below 300. Arthur liked moving back and forth between crafting words and counting them. He liked working within strict boundaries that made him focus less on his fear of writing and more on his desire to win the game. Like whittling away on a branch, he chopped this and cut that, and selected new words and punctuation while doing so, until his piece was not only tighter but also more meaningful.

I had never seen Arthur more excited about writing. For him, the composition process was different from what he was used to. He chose what to write about, talked it out at length, and had it recorded in his authentic voice. A story seemed to travel straight from his brain onto the paper, as if by magic, circumventing the regular hurdles. With that, Arthur's task wasn't to produce words on an empty page—which can feel terrifying for children and adults alike—but to shave down what was already there. Writing as whittling. Writing as a series of choices between words. Writing as erasure.

A number of writing skills are introduced and reinforced by whittling: the skill of replacing inaccurate words with accurate ones; the skill of recognizing and removing repeated words and phrases; the skill of constructing long sentences without letting them become run-ons. Writing skills such as these are taught remarkably well in a writing workshop. Their use organically grows from student activity. Their importance appears naturally to students. Mini-lessons aptly teach and reinforce them as necessary. Just as a student needs straight-cutting skills or his structure will not align and bear weight, a student needs composition skills or the structure of his piece will fall apart.

Literary whittling is not something I learned to do in writing classes. It wasn't until I led writing workshop that I recognized whittling as an activity that applies to writing skills. Now, I show a photo of a woodworker whittling away until a figure emerges, and connect it to what we do in our writing.

Learning and practicing hands-on skills is fundamental to all workshops. It's the whole point. A shop fosters skilled workers of all kinds. A shop forces students to learn by doing. A shop allows learners to develop skills on the spot and sharpen them with repeated use.

As arguments for the writing workshop model emphasize, the technical skills of writing are not ignored in a writing workshop; rather, they are constantly being taught and assessed through mini-lessons and individual conferences. They are constantly being introduced in response to ideas, conversation, peer collaboration, and the writing students produce. We want our students to gain automaticity of mechanics. In a writing shop, students learn and practice mechanics while engaged in the writing process and all the work writers do, often without conscious thought.

Yet, in the writing community, teachers and administrators of writing programs are constantly fed opinion pieces and blog posts asking, "Can writing even be taught?" In the teaching community, writing teachers are faced with the question, "Can writing skills be taught?" And with the growth of the writing workshop model, we are asked, "Can writing skills really be taught in a writing workshop? Without grammar worksheets?"

Many educators remain hesitant to set up writing workshops in their classrooms; they fear skills will be lost amid the choice and varied pacing. They wonder how skills can be strengthened if not tried on worksheets, replicated on homework assignments, and assessed on quizzes. I was one of those teachers. For a brief time, I taught remedial writing to incoming college students. My goal was to cover every skill: word choice, spelling, sentence structure, punctuation, capital letters, paragraph structure, genre selection, figurative writing, and more. Despite my love of workshop, I worried that I would not prepare these students for rigorous coursework, and I fell back on a traditional approach when designing my syllabus. When I shared with my department head my plan for the semester, she upended it by reminding me that writers learn to write by reading good writing and, simply, by writing.

On the other hand, some educators have adopted the process approach—*they'll learn to write by writing*—to such an extent that skills are purposefully sidelined. Skills learning is viewed as oppressive, while nurturing individual expression of each child is the guiding principle. Teachers weigh authentic context heavily, focusing on genre study and devising exciting pieces with real-life applications. Weekly planners list project after project: legend, poem, persuasive essay, book review, letter to a local politician. Pre-writing, with brainstorming worksheets and graphic organizers, takes on a life of its own.

Fortunately, a writing shop runs on a balance of process and skills. Shop is, in fact, the *most* skills-based center of learning. A shop, while allowing students to work on one or more ongoing projects, focuses heavily on skills with its hands-on approach. By closely observing their master, students watch composition skills in action, like sequencing events and including subjects and objects in sentences, and observe how to change course if something goes wrong. By wading through the mess of tools and materials, students practice choosing forms and words that match their ideas and arranging them in an order that is coherent and carries meaning. By having all their senses stimulated, students are led, organically, to attempt figurative writing. By reading drafts to each other and recording themselves, they study the cadence of dialogue and the structure of sentences, while honing in on what makes writing sound more fluid and what makes their voices unique. By constructing paragraphs the way builders construct homes, they face the very real threat of their compositions falling apart and learn how to shore up the structure with strong organization and relevant supporting details. By conferencing with their mentor, they work one-on-one on particular skills, like using quotation marks or choosing the right spelling between words that sound alike. By collaborating with each other, they witness skills other students are already using, and as a group, they help their teacher identify which skills the majority of the class needs to review in mini-lessons. And by doing it all, again and again, students get really good at it all.

In my graduate course on writing workshop, the teachers and I sit with students' writer's notebooks after each shop, poring through their writing, identifying strengths and weakness, listing skills common to all and skills no one has yet understood, let alone mastered. These sessions allow us to track each individual's progress, avoid wasting time teaching mini-lessons on skills the students are already using fluently, identify skills the whole group needs to learn or re-learn, and identify skills individual students can include in their unique set of goals as they write.

In shop, students tend to teach each other new skills. Since all students are not working on identical pieces, many different skills are being deployed at one time. Third-grader Kleydi, for example, mastered the skill of beginning sentences with capital letters. She'd gained automaticity of the skill, no longer needing to consciously think about starting with capitals or editing for them later. Kleydi was revising her piece about a community garden to add details, while next to her Joel was writing about movie theaters. He hadn't capitalized the start of even half the sentences. With the ease and seamlessness so beautifully possible in a writing shop, Kleydi leaned over to help Joel remember the skill and practice it two or three times before returning to her piece.

Kleydi left the brief interaction the way she entered it: confident in her capitalization skill and willing to help a peer. She also got to play master to an apprentice for a moment, without the role being assigned to her. Her organic assumption of the role added to her developing sense of herself as a writer, teacher, and leader.

Joel left the brief interaction with the skill fresh on his mind. Exposed to Kleydi and her writing, Joel now uses the skill again and again in his, as he writes sentences that mean something to him, until the skill becomes automatic. This kind of mastering/apprenticing of skills learning occurs with great frequency in a shop, where the off-page skills of observation and collaboration are always being practiced as much as technical skills.

Technical skills in a shop are also taught and practiced in a growing pattern, so that at any one time, a student is utilizing two or more learned skills: capitalization, punctuation, sentence structure, paragraph organization, planning, editing, and more. I rarely hear a student say she's aware she is practicing skills, the way she does when she's expected to fill out a worksheet. Rather, she's hands-on and wrist-deep in the act of writing. She's capitalizing first words of sentences because at some point in the school year, she absorbed the skill and has been employing it ever since. Skills acquisition is continuous and often cyclical in writing workshop, the way it is in any other shop. Once you learn a skill in shop, you must use it all the time in order to continue building, carving, crafting.

Ralph Fletcher and JoAnn Portalupi (2001) explain such "embedded-skill teaching" and why it succeeds over isolated worksheets (pp. 89–90). In a workshop, where students are writing constantly, "You watch to see what skills kids put to use in their drafts. Your students' writing—their strengths and shortcomings—determines what skills you will teach and when you will teach them" (p. 90). Students, by *doing*, reveal the skills they already have and the skills they need to learn. Skills are the backbone of writing workshop.

I am a professional writer, and I still need to learn and practice new writing skills in my own shop. Not too long ago, I learned that the statement "I feel badly" is incorrect. Since "feel" simply links to the adjective, the sentence should read, "I feel bad." (We would never say, "I feel sadly" or "I feel angrily.") I have to practice this new skill of using linking verbs. I have to say it aloud and write it a few times and keep an index card as a reminder. When I can't write for a while, I sense certain skills growing rusty. I need to triple-check the spelling of words I nearly always spell wrong and remind myself of particular grammar rules that don't seem to stick. (Do I capitalize the first letter after a colon? To the style guides …) Similarly, I learn new teaching moves and need to put them into practice each time I'm in the classroom. And on top of that, I am constantly learning new skills in my kitchen and yard. Learning and practicing skills is not limited to students. We can tap our own skills learning as we guide our students through theirs.

The way I look at writing shop is this: the mess and senses are the parts. The writing process is the power, the gasoline or electricity that makes everything go. But skills are needed to put the thing together. Without parts, power, and knowhow, there's no working machine. I share this with my students. I want them to understand the mechanical nature of writing, to embrace the word "practice" without fearing it the way they often do in conventional writing classrooms. Nick Offerman (2016) says of his woodworking:

> I don't think I've ever picked up a tool and used it successfully on the first try or often even the twentieth try. But on that twenty-first go-around, when I manage to correctly make a shaving cut with a drawknife—well, I feel the very eldritch magic coursing through my musculature and my nifty opposable thumb digits that have allowed us to leave our simian ancestors in the developmental dust. (p. 9)

Writing mechanics can borrow a little of the magic conjured by a running skill saw or a potter's wheel on high speed.

APPRENTICE TO ARTIST

Craft Techniques

> It was as if, through that one sentence, she had wandered out of the yard of her usual language and found herself in a different, mysterious, elegant part of town. (Feinberg, 2011, p. 30)

My friend Claire is an expert editor with degrees in comparative literature and linguistics. While editing a series of essays I co-wrote with our friend Cheryl, Claire had this way of intuiting what needed to be done with a sentence. She could see *how* to rearrange words and change verb tenses, because she could articulate *why* those things needed to be done.

Here's one example. In an essay on greed in the writing community, I first drafted, "In our writing world—which I like to characterize by its celebration of art, encouragement of self-expression, and camaraderie between peers—greed seems to have no place." I knew the sentence was long and clunky, though grammatically correct. It was not smooth but it was not embarrassingly wrong. Claire, however, made this revision: "In our writing world—which celebrates art, self-expression, and camaraderie among peers—greed seems to have no place." Claire explained her thinking in a note to me:

> Edits mostly to eliminate extra words but also because I think 'which I characterize' is not quite what you mean. It suggests you impose these characteristics or imagine them. But I think you mean that the writing life *is characterized by* these qualities, and, furthermore, that you tend to notice the positives and discount the negatives? The edit goes for an active construction that also eliminates words. (C. Guyton, personal communication, October 22, 2012)

She was right. Eliminating the extra words made the sentence read smoothly, and taking "which I characterize" out of the sentence emboldened and generalized the statement. Had Claire simply proofread my piece, the sentence may have stood. But Claire has years of experience turning good, grammatically correct pieces into neat, polished prose. With her experience as an editor and linguistics background, she suggested techniques I could use to elevate my craft.

Beyond the technical skills of writing, the skills that allow students to compose something clear and meaningful with accurate grammar and usage, are the techniques, the specialized moves writers use to lift their writing from mechanically correct to elegant (one might say, to a high degree of craftsmanship). A technique lesson lives in Claire's comments on my sentence and in Arthur's whittling exercise from the previous chapter: good writers eliminate wordiness to make their writing better. Succinct writing is more exciting and enjoyable to read. A writer with skills can still be wordy. But a really good writer, one who has not only polished her skills but also learned techniques of the trade, is not wordy. Writers do this by striking a number of things that show up in a first draft: repeated words and phrases, redundancies, unnecessary synonyms, labels, fillers, wordy phrases, awkward constructions. Each one of those could be taught in isolation with a lesson, worksheet, and homework. But in a shop, these techniques are taught in tandem and in response to student writing.

Matthew Crawford (2009), the think-tank head who left his lucrative job to fix motorcycles, tells the story of his first car, a 1963 Volkswagen Bug. The vehicle gave him freedom from a childhood on a commune, but also gave him headaches as he labored to refurbish it. The 17-year-old Crawford worked not to get the car running, which it was doing just fine, but to get it running at a higher performance level. Faster and smoother. While installing a new motor, Crawford's friend Chas drew on his vast knowledge and experience to diagnose a problem. "Now I saw it," writes Crawford. "Countless times since that day, a more experienced mechanic has pointed out to me something that was right in front of my face, but which I lack the knowledge to see" (p. 91). Crawford further explains what a master like Chas brings to the task. The mechanic's look at a problem is,

> … an active process, bound up with his knowledge of patterns and root causes. Further, his knowledge and perception are bound up with a third thing, which is a kind of ethical involvement. He looks for clues and causes only if he *cares* about the motor, in a personal way. (p. 95)

With Chas's help, Crawford rehabbed his engine. "Rebuilding a motor, then, is more humanly involved than assembling one on an assembly line," he writes. "It is a craft activity" (p. 95).

Just as the expert mechanic knows what makes for a good, quality bike that goes fast and smooth, the expert writer knows what makes for good, quality writing that reads fast and smooth. In the writing shop, craft techniques are as valued as technical skills, because the master cares about the writing, because the students apprentice the master, because the shop prioritizes good writing. Technical skills are necessary for students to write in routine ways, showing the main characteristics of all good writing: organized, clear, original, coherent, and mechanically correct. Craft techniques are necessary for students to write in graceful ways: rhythmic, compelling, powerful.

During one workshop, a student named Bethany, who had previously shown more interest in completion rather than exploration, discovered such a technique. Inspired by a photograph of an older, thick-legged woman with a pipe hanging from her mouth, a photo that was part of the mess of workshop that day, she wrote a short fictional description of the woman, explaining who she was and what her life was like. One sentence read, "She is stubborn as a bull." It's grammatically correct and shows the skills of word order, sentence structure, and figurative speech.

But the woman in the photo demanded something different. Something less cliché, something that could sharply evoke the photo's setting, which looked like it might be a farm. Bethany didn't want to cross out the description, the way we often ask our students to do in favor of a more exciting adjective. She didn't want to let go of the words she felt were important and accurate. Instead, she moved them around the way you might move scraps of fabric around until a quilt comes together. She landed on a new order and, by doing so, invented a new adjective: bull-stubborn. Trying further, Bethany moved the whole sentence around, because it lilted when she said it aloud. With the technique of rearranging, "She is stubborn as a bull" turned into "Bull-stubborn, she is." I still revel in this sentence. Even though "bullheaded" fits, bull-stubborn is an eye- and ear-catcher. I re-read it now and can vividly picture the woman in the photo, stained bonnet crowning her hair, tobacco pipe suspended in her lips. Bull-stubborn indeed.

Importantly, Brittany shared her discovery with others, who began looking for adjectives they might re-invent. Once I noticed her table was buzzing about this newfound technique, I pulled the whole group together to give a very brief, on-the-spot mini-lesson about how we can link nouns and adjectives together with hyphens in order to make more vivid descriptors: rock-hard bread, smoke-thick curtain, lemon-yellow dress. The skill of identifying adjectives and nouns underlies the technique of linking them together in surprising ways.

I don't know that I would have pre-planned that lesson. In fact, I'm sure I wouldn't have. Getting the word order right, identifying the subject and verb, adding an adjective ... those are the lessons. Parts of speech, sentence structure, detail. But Brittany invited her classmates, and invited me as well, to use a new technique, one that contained multiple lessons. Peter Johnston (2012), while discussing the critical importance of how we use language in the classroom, calls the act of teaching "planned opportunism" and says it requires "constant improvisation" (p. 4). Shop is built on opportunism and improvisation. Shop teachers are always in tune with teachable moments.

Third-grader Allyson, a prolific writer, spent the first few minutes of one shop talking about the beach. She spoke what she thought would become her introductory line: "My favorite place is the beach." I asked her why, and she responded, "Since I was born in the summer." We practiced putting the independent and dependent clause together: "My favorite place is the beach, since I was born in the summer." Knowing she already had a handle on sentence structure, which she was demonstrating during our conversation, I asked Allyson to play with the sentence by switching the two clauses around. After two tries, she said, "Since I was born in the summer, my favorite place is the beach." And she smiled. "I like that!" "Me too!" I said. With invented spelling, she started her narrative with the new sentence she and I both felt was interesting. What made it interesting? A craft technique that turned a perfectly ordinary, grammatically correct sentence into something with a little sophistication (see Figure 9.1).

Note the misspelling of "since." In that moment with Allyson, who enjoyed the sound of her newfound sentence, I did not bring up spelling, nor did I launch into an explanation about subordinating conjunctions. Let her sit with her craft. Satisfied with our master/apprentice moment that revolved around a new technique, I did what so often feels counterintuitive: I walked away. The spelling of "since" could be addressed another day.

Fletcher and Portalupi (2001) link the learning of craft techniques directly to safety. They remind us that only in a safe environment can a young writer take a risk with a new technique, especially one that will mark her writing as different from the rest of the writing in the shop (p. 24). And author Natalie Goldberg (1986) says,

> When I teach a class, I want the students to be "writing down the bones," the essential, awake speech of their minds. But I also know I can't just say, "Okay, write clearly and with great honesty." In class we try different techniques or methods. Eventually, the students hit the mark, come home to what they need to say and how they need to say it. (p. 4)

> Singhs I was born in the Summer my favrite place is the beach! When I'm in the beach I hear Kid yelling and screaming and birds cheerping beutfly. The watermelon Smells like sweet Sugar water and the Sea Smells like Salty water. The air Smells like frash air. When I'm at the beach I taste Sweet, soft watermelon and delisions, cold, Smooth Ice cream Which I eat the Ice cream.

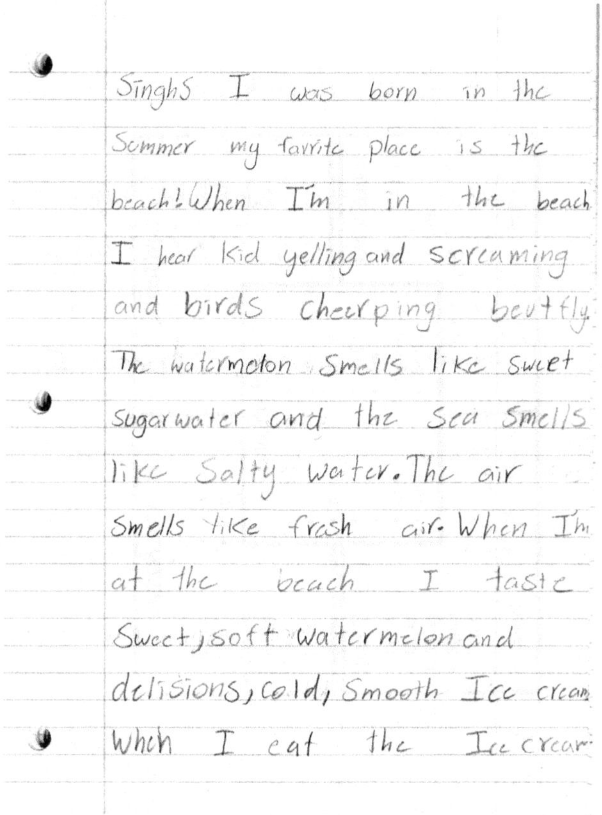

Figure 9.1. Allyson, grade 3, tries a new technique

It's our job as masters to highlight and demonstrate craft techniques. We must notice when techniques are useful to our students and introduce them at appropriate moments. And, critically, we must recognize when our students are already using them. We must stop to shine a light on these techniques and encourage our students to try them out. And we must honor the risk-taking that leads to discovery.

CHAPTER 10

SHARE THE MASTERPIECE

Among my teaching colleagues, I have long been known for classroom management. Logic and organization come naturally to me, and so of all the fundamentals of teaching, classroom management is the one I best understand. To manage a group of students effectively, I recommend that you, "Design your classroom system—organization, routine, ebb and flow of movement—carefully, so your class stays productive, avoids chaos, and remains ready for the unexpected" (Smith, 2018).

As a parent of three young boys, I see evidence of my classroom management at home as well. My boys' routine is strong and clear. Visual cues remind them of the basics, like the day of the week and whose turn it is to put out plates for dinner. They help create the routine, which invests them in following it. We emphasize turn taking, sharing, individual responsibility, family responsibility, transitions, and rules.

Two lessons arise from my management system. The first is my essential motto: *Every rule has a reason.* If I roll out a new policy in the classroom, there has to be a reason to back it up. When one class of boys asked me why they had to take apart their Lego creations after every single free time, I realized I didn't know the answer. So I established a weekly procedure instead, for which I did have a reason. It's both fair and helpful to all students if we say goodbye to our vehicles on Friday, and start fresh with all pieces available on Monday. The same motto applies in parenting. My sons often reply to my guidelines with the simple question, "Why?" If I don't have a reason, the policy breaks down. When one of my twins wanted to sleep with his new basketball, a gift from a friend, my knee-jerk reaction was, "No." Of course, he immediately asked me, "Why not?" I could not think of a reasonable answer. Why not? So he slept with his new ball and no one was worse for it.

Managing final products in a shop should follow the same motto. Every product has a reason. In some shops, it's easy to see the reasons clearly. My sister, in her quilting shop, produces projects that her clients request, like quilts made with the special t-shirts and jerseys of graduating high schoolers.

She allows students to dream up their own final projects based on their interests. They use newfound skills and techniques to create original items that perfectly reflect their personalities.

Figure 10.1. Personal name sign by Lucy, grade 8

My cousin Chris fixes, among other things, vehicles; a project is finished when the vehicle works, performing its intended function. He also makes custom lighting and furniture, such as a table for an avid golfer made with golf clubs and balls (see Figure 10.2).

Figure 10.2. Commissioned golf table, by my cousin Chris

In fact, Chris told me that when crafting the table, he experienced a moment that reminded him of the writing shop: "Interestingly, the top of clubs where I drilled out the golf balls was a point of 'writer's block' for me. It took quite a few nights of dreaming to get that, what turned out to be, a simple solution to mount up the glass. (And several junk golf balls!)" (C. Farrell, personal communication, September 10, 2018).

In shop, however, not all projects need to be completed. That's what tinkering is for. We learn, practice, and play when we tinker. When I was about 15, my mother tried teaching me to sew. We chose a pattern for a sundress and a lightweight fabric. We laid the dress over the pattern and began to pin and cut. That's as far as we got. I learned about selecting, pinning, and cutting. But my homework and boyfriend and after-school activities and job at the store took time away from the unfinished dress. It stayed that way until

I moved my things out of my mother's house and into my own apartment after college. I'd learned by then that I didn't love to sew, nor did I feel guilt for leaving the dress incomplete.

The motto works for publications in the writing shop too. *Every publication has a reason. If there is no reason, don't waste your students' time.* If I consider having all students "finish" a particular piece of writing—give it a title, copy it over as a final draft, illustrate it—I have to ask myself first, why? What is the reason I want this project to be completed? To show my administrator evidence of our efforts? To occupy my students' attention? To please families who want to see a product come home? To satisfy an urge to have *something* finished? If those are my reasons, the publication breaks down, becomes busy work without purpose.

A writing shop should produce relevant final products that naturally flow from the shop activity. Products may be traditional or avant-garde, high-tech or paper-based, solo or collaborative. Projects may be dictated by the students, not by the teacher. Whatever they are, they should have a reason for being.

My shops have produced literary journals, interview magazines, recipe books, poetry collections, newspapers, and hard-cover fiction. They have also produced author biographies, poems written on anything but paper, and plays featuring dialogue between the writers and their inner voices.

Students are involved in the planning and execution of all the publications. In one undergraduate shop, students wrote postcard-length characterizations of familiar people, because they wanted to practice extremely short descriptive writing and get to know their subjects while doing so. In one second-grade shop, in which classmates were especially companionable, students mailed letters to each other explaining in detail why they liked each other so much. In a graduate shop, students wrote notes to their former selves as a means to better understand their own young students.

My shops have also produced lists: What makes good writing? What makes a writer? What are all the kinds of writing we've seen out in the world? What kinds of writing do we produce every single day, often without realizing it? In other words, we publish writing on writing.

Shops produce tips of the trade. Shops produce public readings. Shops produce interactive websites. Shops produce buddies who read their finished stories to younger students. Shops produce new masters of craft. Shops produce a writing community.

I also like to think of the writing shop itself as a masterpiece. Like a well-outfitted garage or state-of-the-art test kitchen, like my mother's sewing studio that boasted a perfect place for each tiny thing, like my father's basement workshop that housed a tool for every job, a writing shop itself is something to be admired. Students and their master make a shop together, filling it with the tools and materials they need to build. Before long, the shop is bustling, with its mess, sense stimulation, workspace variety, and safety procedures. Technical skills and craft techniques are learned and practiced. The shop is a product of hard work, a living publication that features the interests and personalities of so many young writers.

And here is the second lesson from my classroom management system, one that took me years to learn: *You can't plan for everything*. No matter how organized you are, something may get lost. No matter how much you emphasize safety, someone may get hurt. When I taught English and music to students at a rural school in Costa Rica one summer, I was given a list of qualities I should bring to the classroom. Along with engagement, love, and persistence when teaching across languages and cultures, was this: "tolerance to uncertainty and a sense of humor." Things go awry. Paint spills. Smile and work through it.

My son's genetic syndrome presents as a number of symptoms, from core weakness to fine-motor delays. He is sensitive to temperature. Food, playground equipment, and car seats can't be too warm. The freezer aisle at the grocery store is frustratingly cold. Over his spring break, I took him to a water park for the first time. He was nervous. But when he saw his brothers ride a waterslide, he decided he wanted to try it too. So I took him on my lap. He clung to me, fingernailing my forearms, as we accelerated down the serpentine slide.

My experience of the ride was this: My neck hurt from holding my son upright, my elbows got banged up from keeping us level through the sharp turns, my lungs ingested too much water as I took the brunt of the landing.

My son's experience of the ride was this: He tried something new. He felt brave. He had fun. He was a little scared, but in the end, nothing bad happened to either one of us. He told the story over and over for days.

Writing shop, like any shop, is not tightly controlled. It's a little looped, a little loose. Managing shop bangs up our elbows. But the benefits, at the bottom, are profound. An uncertain ride is far more transformative than a scripted one. So long as a writer has a guide, feels safe to take the plunge, and has learned something new by the end, an uncertain ride is worth it. And however you land is a direct result of how the ride went on the way down.

Remember that every publication has a reason. And remember that you can't plan for everything. Remember that writing shop is, at heart, a dynamic workshop where we build meaningful things.

You can master a shop, bruised elbows and all.

REFERENCES

Anderson, C. (2000). *How's it going? A practical guide to conferring with student writers.* Portsmouth, NH: Heinemann.

Bazerman, C. (2016). What do sociocultural studies of writing tell us about learning to write? In C. MacArthur, S. Graham, & J. Fitzgerald (Eds.), *Handbook of writing research* (2nd ed., pp. 11–23). New York, NY: The Guilford Press.

Bertin, P., & Perlman, E. (1998). *Preventing academic failure: A multisensory curriculum for teaching reading, spelling and handwriting in the elementary classroom* (12th ed.). Retrieved from http://www.PAFprogram.com

Calkins, L. (1994). *The art of teaching writing.* Portsmouth, NH: Heinemann.

Christakis, E. (2017). *The importance of being little: What young children really need from grownups.* New York, NY: Penguin.

Corgill, A. M. (2008). *Of primary importance: What's essential in teaching young writers.* Portland, ME: Stenhouse.

Crawford, M. (2009). *Shop class as soul craft: An inquiry into the value of work.* New York, NY: Penguin.

Cruz, C. (2008). *A quick guide to reaching struggling writers.* Portsmouth, NH: Heinemann.

Cumming, A. (2016). Writing development and instruction for English language learners. In C. MacArthur, S. Graham, & J. Fitzgerald (Eds.), *Handbook of writing research* (2nd ed., pp. 364–376). New York, NY: The Guilford Press.

Cunningham, K. (2009). The power of words. *Saint David's Magazine*, p. 11.

DeSalvo, L. (2014). *The art of slow writing: Reflections on time, craft, and creativity.* New York, NY: St. Martin's Griffin.

Dillard, A. (1998). To fashion a text. In W. Zinsser (Ed.), *Inventing the truth: The art and craft of memoir* (pp. 141–161). New York, NY: Mariner Books.

Dufilho-Rosen, K. (Producer), & Eggleston, R. (Director). (2000). *For the birds* [Motion picture]. Emeryville, CA: Pixar.

Feinberg, B. (2011). Ruby: On not editing children. *Teachers & Writers*, 30–31.

Fletcher, R., & Portalupi, J. (2001). *Writing workshop: The essential guide.* Portsmouth, NH: Heinemann.

Frazier, I. (1995). Looking for my family. In W. Zinsser (Ed.), *Inventing the truth: The art and craft of memoir* (pp. 163–181). New York, NY: Mariner Books.

Freymann, S., & Elffers, J. (1999). *How are you peeling? Foods with moods.* New York, NY: Arthur A. Levine Books.

Fu, D., & Shelton, N. (2007, March). Including students with special needs in a writing workshop. *Language Arts, 84*(4), 325–336.

Goldberg, N. (1986). *Writing down the bones.* Boston, MA: Shambhala Publications.

Gopnik, A. (Speaker), & Vedantam, S. (Host). (2017, December 11). *Hidden brain* [Audio podcast]. Retrieved from http://www.npr.org

Graves, D. (1983). *Writing: Teachers & children at work.* Portsmouth, NH: Heinemann.

Harwayne, S. (2000). *Lifetime guarantees: Toward ambitious literacy teaching.* Portsmouth, NH: Heinemann.

REFERENCES

James, K., Jao, R. J., & Berninger, V. (2016). The development of multileveled writing systems of the brain: Brain lessons for writing instruction. In C. MacArthur, S. Graham, & J. Fitzgerald (Eds.), *Handbook of writing research* (2nd ed., pp. 116–129). New York, NY: The Guilford Press.

Jauss, D. (2008). *Alone with all that could happen: Rethinking conventional wisdom about the craft of fiction writing*. Cincinnati, OH: Writer's Digest Books.

Johnson, B. (2011, October 11). *How we spend our days: Barb Johnson* [Web log interview]. Retrieved from https://catchingdays.cynthianewberrymartin.com

Johnston, P. (2012). *Opening minds: Using language to change lives*. Portland, ME: Stenhouse.

Kinloch, V., & Burkhard, T. (2016). Teaching writing in culturally and linguistically diverse classrooms. In C. MacArthur, S. Graham, & J. Fitzgerald (Eds.), *Handbook of writing research* (2nd ed., pp. 377–391). New York, NY: The Guilford Press.

Klassen, J. (2012). *This is not my hat*. Somerville, MA: Candlewick Press.

Lee, S. (2008). *Wave*. San Francisco, CA: Chronicle Books.

Leffel, C., & Mandler, C. (Eds.). (2016). *The best salon essays*. New York, NY: Editors.

Lewis, B. (Producer), & Bird, B. (Director). (2007). *Ratatouille* [Motion picture]. Emeryville, CA: Pixar.

Mars, R. (Host), & Greenspan, S. (Producer). (2016, December 12). *99% invisible* [Audio podcast]. Retrieved from https://99percentinvisible.org

Martone, M. (2012, April 12). Catching one's breath: Longevity, endurance, interval training, and the hypoxic workshop. *TriQuarterly*. Retrieved from http://www.triquarterly.org

McClanahan, R. (2001). *Write your heart out: Exploring & expressing what matters to you*. Cincinnati, OH: Walking Stick Press.

McCourt, F. (1998). Learning to chill out. In W. Zinsser (Ed.), *Inventing the truth: The art and craft of memoir* (pp. 61–81). New York, NY: Mariner Books.

Miller, B., & Paola, S. (2005). *Tell it slant: Writing and shaping creative nonfiction*. New York, NY: McGraw-Hill.

Morrison, T. (1998). The site of memory. In W. Zinsser (Ed.), *Inventing the truth: The art and craft of memoir* (pp. 183–200). New York, NY: Mariner Books.

Mraz, K., Porcelli, A., & Tyler, C. (2016). *Purposeful play: A teacher's guide to igniting deep and joyful learning across the day*. Portsmouth, NH: Heinemann.

Murray, D. (1985). *A writer teaches writing*. Boston, MA: Houghton Mifflin.

Offerman, N. (2016). *Good clean fun: Misadventures in sawdust at Offerman Woodshop*. New York, NY: Dutton.

Pryle, M. (2012). *Writing workshop in middle school*. New York, NY: Scholastic.

Ray, K. W. (2001). *Writing workshop: Working through the hard parts (and they're all hard parts)*. Urbana, IL: National Council of Teachers of English.

Ritvo, M. (Speaker), & Harris, M. (Host). (2016, July 12). *Only human* [Audio podcast]. Retrieved from http://www.wnyc.org

Robbins, M., King, C., & Sung, E. (2017). *Breakfast, lunch, dinner, life ...: Recipes and adventures from my home kitchen*. New York, NY: Rizzoli International Publications.

Schwartz, K. (2016). *I wish my teacher knew: How one question can change everything for our kids*. Boston, MA: Da Capo Press.

Shannon, D. (1998). *No, David!* New York, NY: Blue Sky Press.

Silverman, S. W. (2009). *Fearless confessions: A writer's guide to memoir*. Athens, GA: The University of Georgia Press.

Smith, S. F. (2018). What are your teaching fundamentals? *Edutopia*. Retrieved from http://www.edutopia.org

Stonebrink, B. (2001). An opportunity on Elm Street. *Willamette Journal*. Retrieved from http://www.nwp.org

Tannenbaum, J., & Bush, V. C. (2005). *Jump write in! Creative writing exercises for diverse communities, grades 6–12*. San Francisco, CA: Jossey-Bass.

Unferth, D. O. (2016, March 28). Draft. *Wigleaf*. Retrieved from http://www.wigleaf.com

Weiss, N. (1991). *Surprise box*. New York, NY: Putnam.

Williams, R. [Prince Ea]. (2016, September 26). *The people vs. the school system* [Video file]. Retrieved from https://youtu.be/dqTTojTija8

Williams, T. T. (1996). An unspoken hunger. In J. Kitchen & M. P. Jones (Eds.), *In short: A collection of brief creative nonfiction* (p. 44). New York, NY: W. W. Norton.

ABOUT THE AUTHOR

Suzanne Farrell Smith is a writer, editor, and teacher. Her work explores education, parenthood, memory, trauma, and the writing life, and appears in numerous literary and scholarly journals. She is the author of *The Memory Sessions*, a memoir without memory, forthcoming from Bucknell University Press. A Connecticut native, Suzanne graduated from Trinity College and moved to Manhattan, where she taught elementary school. She spent summers, holiday breaks, and after-school hours working with students in under-performing schools, students in rural Costa Rica, and students in crisis. With master's degrees from The New School and Vermont College of Fine Arts, she now teaches writing workshops as well as undergraduate and graduate courses on literacy education. After 16 city years, she moved back to Connecticut, where she lives in a creek-cut valley with her husband and three sons.

Printed in the United States
By Bookmasters